EXCELLENCE BY DESIGN

JON D. VREDEVOOGD
Michigan State University

KENDALL/HUNT PUBLISHING COMPANY
2460 Kerper Boulevard P.O. Box 539 Dubuque, Iowa 52004-0539

This edition has been printed directly from camera-ready copy.

ISBN 0-8403-8886-1

Printed in the United States of America
10 9 8 7 6 5 4 3 2 1

Foreword

EXCELLENCE BY DESIGN

I met Jon D. Vredevoogd in 1976 when we were both faculty members at Michigan State University. He was teaching design and I was a clinician researcher in Biomechanics. I heard from one of his students that he believed that Nature made the best designs, that Nature was the best problem solver, that everything Nature designed was done as it was done for specific purposes and that to be most efficient in design and problem solving we should all study Nature's designs first.

Since that time, Jon and I have spent many hours together helping each other understand natural design and working at problem solving. I have found Jon to be a most direct and effective problem solver. He seldom loses focus on the problem under consideration, and he never stops until he develops an effective solution.

Most of our work together has been related to the effects of the environment on health, work efficiency and the like. He is one designer that is extremely well versed in physiology, psychology, the effects of the physical environment on health, mood and efficiency as well as what can be done to improve the conditions in which we work, play, and rest.

This book is well worth the effort required to absorb its contents. Jon leads you by the hand through the process of learning to improve your space so that you will lead a healthier and happier life. It is a privilege to introduce him to you.

John E. Upledger, D.O., O.M.N.
Palm Beach Gardens, Florida

Preface

There are many books on the market today about "Excellence." Most of these describe the habits and talents of people who have achieved excellence in their own lives. However, the difficulty in discussing excellence is not in defining the word or describing the abilities needed to achieve it; rather, the difficulty in discussing excellence is in finding a common language so that everyone can become involved.

This book explains the **concepts** of excellence in the **language** of design, so that it can be applied by the businessperson, the student, the physician, or the engineer. In fact, **anyone** who wants to achieve excellence can use the principles contained in **Excellence by Design** to become more productive.

The concepts of design allow you to discuss excellence and work to achieve excellence in all you do. Design is both a form of thinking and a form of communication. Design affects your ability to function effectively, it becomes a motivator for you, and can even direct you on a subconscious level to the goals you want to achieve.

Excellence cannot be achieved without structure. Design is the process of providing organization and meaning to our lives. Peoples' lives would be enhanced greatly if they would incorporate design concepts into the things they are trying to achieve.

Design is not just for "designers". We "design" every day, in every project we undertake. The difficulty is that most people will not approach the process of design, because they are unfamiliar with it.

This is what **Excellence by Design** is all about.

In order to understand what is so unique about **Excellence by Design**, an overview of the "traditional" process of design versus the process described in this book will be helpful.

In its simplest form, each design proceeds through three phases; the preliminary design phase, the final design phase, and the construction phase. These phases are shown in the leftmost column on the page at the end of this preface.

A more detailed tracking of a design project is represented in the center column. This begins with the CONTRACT and ends with PROJECT COMPLETION. The tracking shows that more than task is taking place at the same time. The REVIEWs represent the presentations and meetings with the client.

The right column shows the various phases of the design process described in **Excellence by Design** and their relationship to the traditional design process. It is not the intent of **Excellence by Design** to replace the traditional process, but to help you to understand the process and indicate where you would want to be involved in the process when working with a professional designer.

You will notice that the phase "You" and the phase "Evaluation" do not appear in the traditional process, but are an integral part of **Excellence by Design**. Also please note that **Excellence by Design** does not cover every nuance of the design process. The complete process is well understood by professional designers and is described in many other excellent books.

Instead, **Excellence by Design** points out the critical elements of the traditional design process and adds to these the phases called "You" and "Evaluation" to provide a better method of approaching design. In doing this, **Excellence by Design** provides designers, business professionals, students, and others with the tools they need to be effective in all they do.

A Comparison Of Traditional Design Phases With The Phases Described In This Book

In its simplest form each design progresses through three phases; the preliminary design phase, the final design phase, and the construction phase. These phases are shown in the left column of page 4.

A more detailed tracking of a design project is represented in the center column. This is shown to begin with the CONTRACT and end with the PROJECT COMPLETION. The tracking shows that more than one task is taking place at the same time. The REVIEWS represent the presentations and meetings with the client.

The right hand column shows the phases described in this book and their relationship to the traditional design process. It is not the intent of this book to replace the traditional process but to help you understand the process and where you would want to be involved in the process when you are working with a professional designer.

You will notice that the phases "You" does not appear in the traditional process. I would also draw your attention to the fact that this book does not cover every nuance of the design process. The process is well understood by professional designers and is described in many other excellent books.

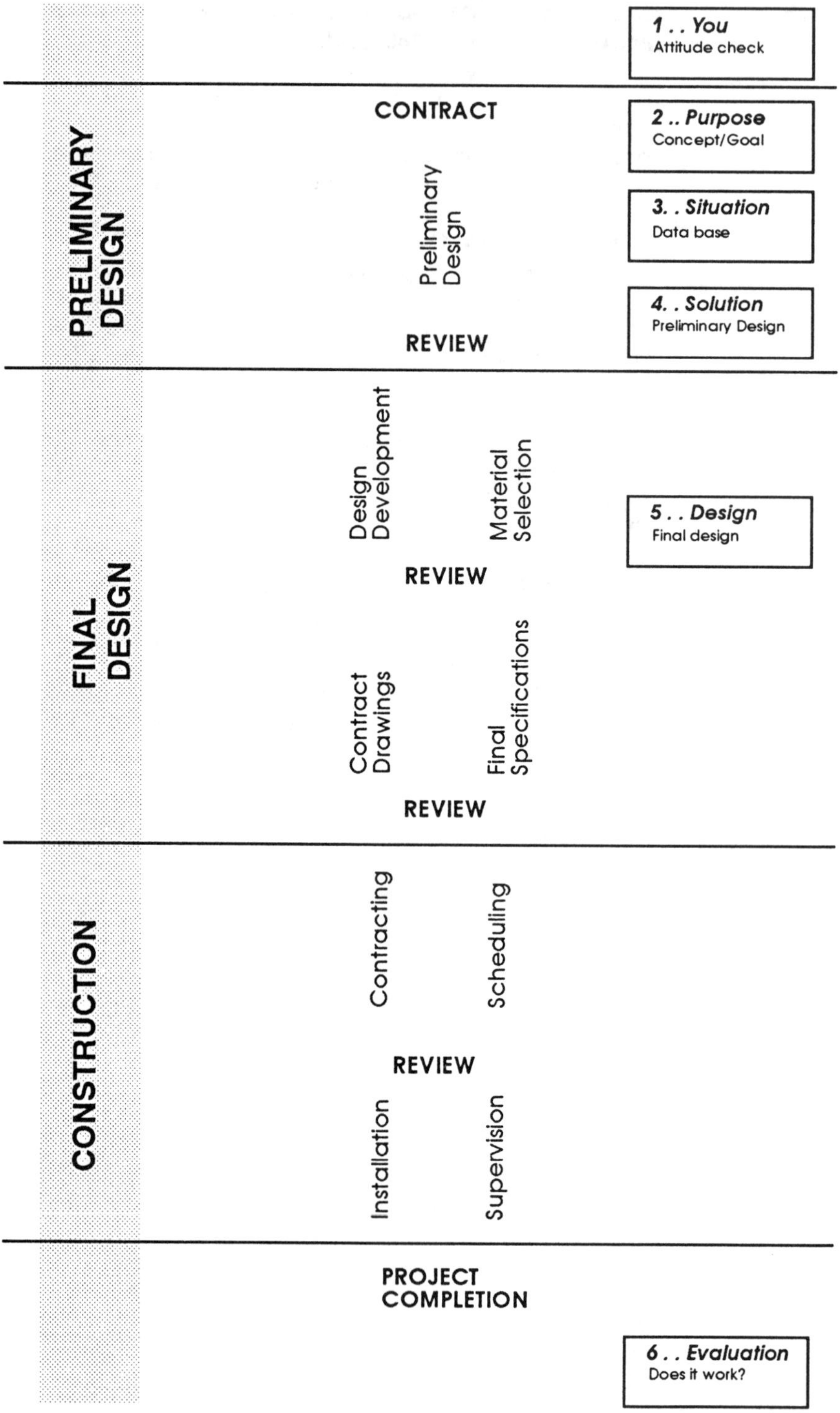
1 . . You
Attitude check
PRELIMINARY DESIGN
CONTRACT
Preliminary Design
REVIEW
2 .. Purpose
Concept/Goal
3. . Situation
Data base
4. . Solution
Preliminary Design
FINAL DESIGN
Design Development
Material Selection
REVIEW
5 . . Design
Final design
Contract Drawings
Final Specifications
REVIEW
CONSTRUCTION
Contracting
Scheduling
REVIEW
Installation
Supervision
PROJECT COMPLETION
6 . . Evaluation
Does it work?

Contents

CHAPTER 1

Everybody designs

The purpose of this book is to remove the confusion, intimidation, stress, and uncertainty many of you experience when someone asks you to express your opinion about a "design". In the broadest sense each of us are designing all the time. When you selected your clothing today, combed your hair, (or didn't), you were designing. In that sense design is neither new or mysterious. Yet, if you analyze what really happens when you design something you will find that designing is a highly complex, multi-leveled and multifaceted process.

As your understanding of design and the design process becomes more familiar, you will find yourself consciously participating more and more in this challenging activity. Design will provide you with another avenue of thinking and expression.

As you read this book, the thoughts that come to you will be more important than the words on the page. This book is about design. It's about thinking, living, and communicating. As you read, record your thoughts. Use the large left hand margin provided for you. Make notes of the various design influences you recognize as you read.

Design terminology

The confusion surrounding design seems to begin with the design terminology. You will find that many of the terms we use can be interpreted as either a noun or a verb.

For example: When I say "design", what comes to your mind? Many people think of a favorite painting, a car, a house, or some other design object. They are thinking of design as a thing (a noun). At the same time others will be thinking about the process of designing (a verb). So, when you say "design", are you talking about the thing or the action?

Share the same perspective

Gestalt psychologists point out that the first requisite in perception is the separation of the object you are looking at from the ground it is seen against. I prefer to substitute the term "context" for the term "ground". Others may refer to it as the surroundings or the environment.

Confusion can occur when you talk about the context of the design because what one person sees as the design object the other may see as the design context. For the fashion designer the clothing is the design object and the body is the design context but for the physician the body is the design object and the clothing is the design context.

The meaning is learned

You may also feel intimidated if you think that you are supposed to understand the meaning of a design without any assistance. The fact is that you need to be taught what the design means. This is one of the roles of designers as well as parents, teachers, advertsers, peers, and others. They explain the meaning of the perfume, the automobile, the fishing pole, etc.

Design is a non-verbal language

Even designers often have difficulty talking about the meaning of their designs. Part of this is a communication problem and part of it is a translation problem. To ask the designer to describe his work is like asking you to describe the taste of steak. You find yourself at a loss for words because it doesn't fit well into words.

Taste is its own language as is smell, painting, and sculpture.

Images, the bases of memory systems

Nonetheless, designs can be powerful tools of communication. Because they can function as powerful reminders, companies hire graphic designers to create images or logos which represent the mission statement of the company.

Intuitively, you know how to design already

You and I are sending and receiving these design messages all the time. It can be fascinating to observe the use of this non-verbal language. Students in my class at Michigan State University never come to class in a business suit unless they have a job interview after the class. The clothes they wear are a statement of their perception of the class and their role in it. They all dress pretty much alike. You might say that they are a part of the group called "students". At the same time they don't want to look exactly like anyone else. They desire to be recognized as unique individuals.

Because we are all involved in sending and receiving these non-verbal messages all the time, it makes sense to understand how to use this language more effectively.

To begin let's separate '***the design***' (the noun form of the word "design") from '***the design process***' (the verb form of the word "design).

When I use the term "*the design*" in this book I am referring to a designed object. This designed object is both a tool and a language.

Consider the example of an automobile. As a tool an automobile extends your ability to move from one place to another farther and faster than you could if you had to walk. As a language, the make and model of the vehicle will trigger thoughts and associations. A Jeep may remind you of all-terrain travel while a Rolls-Royce may give you images of a wealthy owner. Just seeing an automobile like the first one you ever drove may unleash a host of memories.

THE DESIGN AS A TOOL

As a tool and change agent, each design is intended to extend your physical, mental, and spiritual abilities. Physically, it may help you move faster or work better. It may help you organize your papers or tools. Mentally, it may help you remember things. It may help you better understand yourself, and/or better understand your relationship to the universe. It may even stimulate your subconscious.

The tool as a director

When a designer locates the door in a building it determines where you can enter that building. When a designer locates a window in a building it determines what you can and cannot see outside that building. The first thing you see in the morning and the last thing you see at night has been influenced by design. Design objects are very powerful tools used by the designer to control a flow of events and impressions.

Every design has this kind of power, which can be used to help or hinder. The responsibility for its use lies in the hands of the user. Design is a powerful influence in each of our lives.

The tool as a means

It is very easy to make the error of thinking that the design object is the goal of the designer, but it's not. The design is simply the tool that helps us achieve a larger purpose. Everything is directed to "the person response".

Some people think that the architect's drawing is the design. It's really not. It is simply a tool to help in the construction of the building. The only purpose for the building is as a tool or stimulus to help people improve. That is the ultimate result: THE PERSON RESPONSE. Everything that precedes this response is a tool. Recognize that you too are a design in the larger scheme of things. You are a tool or stimulus of your own making.

THE DESIGN AS A LANGUAGE

Design is a very powerful non-verbal language that instructs and directs people without words. Think of the last time you came into a new theater or classroom. You knew where you, as part of the audience, were supposed to sit and where the teacher or the performers were supposed to be. Without a word, the design directed you.

The language influences decisions

Researchers tell us that up to 90% of the decisions sighted people make are based on what they see. That means that 90% of your decisions are based on your ability to understand and correctly interpret visual images. Obviously, it's very important to know how to interpret what you see or should I say "think" you see. People have said "Seeing is believing" or "I know that's true, I've seen it for myself".

Be careful! Remember the last time you went to a magic show? If you based your decisions on what you thought you saw, you would have been wrong. We need to learn to properly interpret what we see and judge when our eyes are deceiving us.

The language expresses the designer

Every design is a reflection of the designer who created it. Therefore, each design gives you insight into the designer. No one can design without communicating a lot about themselves. The design tells you what the designer thought about and by inference what he rejected or did not consider. It tells you what he knows or doesn't know, what he thought important and what he thought wasn't. The design will never be better than the designer. At its very best, it encompasses all the designer understands about the materials, the technology, philosophy, and life itself. Picasso is reported to have made the comment that a person shouldn't paint before the age of 40 because they don't know enough about life to tell someone else how to do it.

Everything you and I do, every design we create is both an expression of ourselves and an influence on others.

I am convinced that if you understand the designer you will have a better understanding of the design because the design is an extension of the designer. Although people say that form follows function, form more significantly follows the designer. This is the reason you can recognize the designer's work. No matter how hard you try to remain unattached, you express yourself in the decisions you make while coordinating the design process.

Because no two people are alike and no two problems are alike, no two designs are ever alike. The next time you look at a design, recognize the uniqueness of the design and the uniqueness of the person behind the design. No one has to work at being unique or creating unique designs. You are already unique, and your designs will inevitably be unique.

The message of the language is learned

As a design student, I remember how intimidated I was by design. I would go to the museum with a friend who would look at a painting and say "look at the emotion in that painting". I didn't see it. Have you ever had this experience? I thought there must be something wrong with me. I'd think to myself, I'm probably the only one in the world that doesn't see that. I was always trying to figure out what was right. I would think, "If only there was a dictionary or perhaps an instruction manual that I could go to, to tell me what it means." No such manual exists, and here is the reason:

There are only two ways to understand a design. Either someone tells you what it means, or you relate it to a past experience you have had with a similar design. That's it! There are no other ways by which you can understand the meaning of a design. That's why there are advertising agencies and owners' manuals. Their purpose is to teach you the meaning they want applied to the new product.

This is very important! I repeat, this is very important! Once meaning has been applied to the design, it is very difficult - if not impossible - to apply a different meaning to that design. Once you have been taught that a VW bug automobile means economical it is very difficult to associate it with luxury.

That's only part of it. If I don't tell you what the design means, you will apply your own meaning. That meaning will be based on your past experience with a similar design. Since your past experiences will be different from everyone else's (because their experiences have been different than yours), the meaning to you will be different from the meaning to others. It is logical then that your interpretation will be different from theirs. In fact, it's to be expected.

Every design object starts without meaning. We assign the meaning we have learned or experienced. Therefore, no design can continue without meaning.

An example of assigning meaning

To demonstrate the dynamics of applying meaning, let me relate to you a situation I observed at the university. Several years ago, the chair of our department had a situation that provided some unexpected one-time money. She wanted to take advantage of the situation to introduce the faculty to computer technology, so she came to each of the faculty and asked "How would you like to have a computer?". The typical response was one of skepticism. Why are you giving me a computer? You have never given me anything like this before. Are you planning to reduce the secretarial staff? Do you think I'm not working hard enough? Obviously, it didn't seem to sell very well. She then came back with a second offer. "If you get a computer you will need a new chair. Here's a catalog, what would you like?" By now, intimidation and anxiety were running very high. What should you say? One by one, the faculty signed up for the computer and the furniture. I have observed as much as two years later that computers in some offices have yet to be turned on. That's an example of people assigning their own meaning.

How could it have happened? The chair might have simply first called a meeting and said to the faculty, "I've come upon some unexpected money, and I've spent time thinking about how I could help make your job a little easier and let you know how much you are appreciated. It came to my attention that computer technology might be an answer. So I would like to make a computer available to you. This equipment will require a place to set in your office, and I have the funds to cover that too. Why don't your select from the catalog what you like?"

Had she done it this way, I am convinced that the response would have been substantially different. The faculty would have been far more receptive. The meaning of the design would have been concern rather than intimidation.

If you are looking for change in your organization, begin with an idea or change in direction and back it up with a change in design. Experience has shown that if you change the design without changing the direction, little or no increase in productivity is seen. If you change the direction without changing the design, little or no change is seen. If you first introduce the change in direction, and then back it up with a change in design, the best results will be seen.

The message is a directive

Throughout history, design has been very effectively used to give us a sense of place by reminding us of our relationship to the universe.

The pyramid isn't just an object or a tomb for the pharaoh; it is a clear statement to the Egyptian on the street that the Pharaoh is a god to him. To stand at the base of the pyramid is to create a sense of awe and to remind him of his insignificance in relation to the pharaoh. In our culture, cathedrals, mosques, and synagogues make a similar statement about our relationship to God.

When you go about your activities today, look at the many ways you are being directed by design. When you enter a bank, how do you know where you are supposed to go, how do you know where you are allowed to go and where you don't belong? I would remind you that you already know how to read many of the visual cues designers use. Now, think about some of the designs you own. What do they say about your place in society? What do they say about your purpose in life? What do you want them to say about you?

The aesthetic is a statement

You might be thinking, "What about beauty? I thought design was about creating beautiful things". Beauty is an aspect of the design. In fact every profession has it's expression of beauty. When designers talk about beauty they use the term "aesthetic" as do the philosophers. Philosophers talk about aesthetic in terms of thought-provoking and non-thought-provoking forms. What they are saying is this: From their point of view, to be beautiful, the design must cause you to think.

I remember interviewing a great architect .one day and asking him. "What are you trying to do with your designs?" He said, "I want my designs to cause a sense of wonder, I want them to tantalize the senses". That could certainly fit the definition of causing you to think. Aesthetic has to do with the thoughts and emotions that are triggered by the design.

Beauty is the exception. It attracts our attention by being different and it holds our attention by the contemplation it elicits.

Beauty is the physical, emotional, and spiritual release you experience when you are presented with a physical representation of all your hopes and dreams.

EVALUATING THE DESIGN

Every design object can be evaluated based on the idea (the concept, or the thought which we will talk about later as the "solution") and the language which is the design itself. You can evaluate every design on the merit of the idea, and also on the design's ability to communicate the idea.

Any design can be evaluated using concept and communication, as follows: One of the results of Albert Einstein's relativistic physics is the notion that mass and energy are really the same. He expressed it with the following mathematical formula. "$E=mc^2$"

Using the matrix below, how would you evaluate his design?

1 - Good idea, poorly communicated
2 - Good idea, clearly communicated
3 - Poor idea, clearly communicated
4 - Poor idea, poorly communicated.

Fit versus flexibility

An ongoing challenge for both the designer and the user is fit vs. flexibility. In general, the design that solves many problems solves none as well as a design that solves only one specific problem. If you have ever used a pocket knife that includes a scissors, a screwdriver, etc. you have found that a "real" screwdriver works better.

Here is the situation to the extreme. If someone designed a perfect coat for you, that coat would meet your physical, mental, and emotional needs. It would be the perfect size for that day, it would fit your mood, and it would meet the specific requirements for that occasion perfectly. The moment the function was over, or your mood changed, or your size changed, the design would be obsolete. The more accurate the design, the shorter the function life.

If we design something less specific, like an all-purpose television antenna, it will bring in lots of stations but it won't do as good a job as an antenna designed to bring in a single channel.

Architects have said that the only buildings that last are bad buildings. They solve lots of problems "sort of," but none well. One can be much more specific in the design of a float for a parade than one can be for a rental trailer. Designers have taken this to the extreme. Some designers attempt to design for the perfect fit of an office space, while others simply provide an enclosure.

Inanimate versus living

It is a challenge to design an inanimate object to meet the needs of a living system. This is really the challenge of putting two things together that are changing at different rates.

This is like trying to put glass and aluminum together. The glass in the window expands and contracts in response to temperature changes at a different rate than the aluminum frame. This presents a problem that can be solved with a rubber gasket that can accommodate the changes.

The same type of phenomenon happens when we put a person in a building. The needs of the person may change more rapidly than the building. Therefore, your design needs to pay heed to human requirements for change as well as physical specifications.

EVALUATING THE DESIGN LANGUAGE

When you evaluate the use of the design language you are evaluating whether or not the idea of the design has been clearly or unclearly stated.

You may find that a good idea is rejected because it is unclearly stated. An example of this might be the design of an inexpensive folding chair that falls apart after you get it home. The idea of an inexpensive folding chair is good, but the frustration of trying to work with the design makes it unsuccessful.

You could have a poor idea that is embellished to look good in spite of the idea. Let's take the example of the cigarette. We all know the health hazards of smoking, yet the way the design is communicated encourages thousands of cigarettes to be sold each year.

You could have a good idea that is clearly stated. An example might be the paper clip. It's a good idea to have something to bind papers together. The paper clip is a clear statement of how it can be accomplished.

There are of course poor ideas that are poorly stated. We can all come up with examples in this category. The "New Coke" concept could be cited as an example of a product that may not have been needed and was ineffectively introduced .

The Design Process

To this point we have been talking about the design object, now let's discuss haow the design object comes about.

The design is the necessary result of *the design process*. You could think about it this way. If I take in my hand a ball of clay and push my thumb into the center or it, the clay would take the form of a dish. I didn't design a dish. The dish was the necessary result of the force I applied to the clay material in the environment of my hand. I selected the material, I established the environment, I applied the force and the dish was the result. If I had changed the force, the environment, or the material I would have changed the result.

The designs we see, whatever they are, are the result of decisions that designers made. Remember that each of us are designers, we all are making decisions every day. You are the result of your genes (the material), your environment and the decisions (the forces) that you have made in your life. What you will become is the result of the decisions you are now making.

Designers are decision makers

People think that the designer is attempting to create objects. The fact is that the designer is making decisions that result in the object. Do you see the difference?

Decisions from Tuning

Designers' decisions are also the result of a tuning process. We have all seen pictures of the artist standing before his easel. He looks at the painting, he looks at the model, he stands back, he thinks, and then he applies some paint or makes some change. What's going on here? I like to describe this as a process of tuning. The artist is making changes in the design until they feel right to him. When it feels right to him, he stops.

You can observe yourself making changes in yourself until it feels right to you. You are using this same tuning process. The result is the design called "You". Your decisions are highly influenced by changes in your physical and emotional environment. If you feel like you are driving well over the speed limit you may be nervous about getting a ticket so you slow down. That's tuning. You feel hungry so you eat. That's tuning. You make decisions based on tuning all the time. This is the same thing the designer and artist does.

A guide for others

When we design for others we are simply the individual who helps gather relevant information that others will tune to. We help organize and prioritize the information that will result in a visual form. The designer is the coordinator of the process, the communicator, and the translator.

An analysis of the design process

In Chapters 2, 3, and 4, I will describe the three skills that are necessary in the design process. In Chapters 5 through 10, I will describe the phases of the design process. Chapters 11 through 13 will describe in detail how to apply the three skills in each of the six phases to design your personal life, to design your workspace, and to design your career.

The rewards will be in direct proportion to your understanding and application of the materials.

An overview of the design process follows.

3 design skills

There are three skills that are applied again and again in the design process. These three skills are already familiar to you since everybody uses them. They include: The skill of gathering relevant data, the skill of organizing and synthesizing that data, and the skill of testing and validating the conclusions.

These skills are used in a cyclical fashion. The cycle may need to be repeated several times in the process. FIGURE 1 illustrates the cycle.

FIGURE 1 The Design Skills

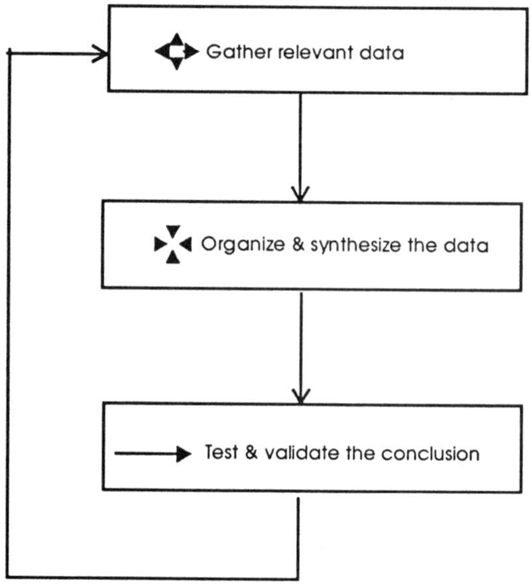

Gather relevant data

You begin by gathering relevant data.

The decisions you will make will never be better than the data you base them on.

If you have no new input you will have no new answers.

Organize and synthesize the data

You will reduce the data to a manageable size because you are always working with time restrictions.

Because your mind compares facts one at a time, you will need to prioritize the data.

Because the design will evolve from a single issue, the challenge is to find the controlling issue or purpose.

Test and validate the conclusion

You will test and validate your conclusion for two reasons:

1. To reduce time and associated costs of error (the "ripple effect").

2. To provide stopping points that can prevent the necessity of starting completely over.

6 design phases

I find that the design process can be divided into six phases after you think there is a need to bring about some change.

If you recognize these phases it's because each of us uses the same problem solving process and simply adjusts it for our own professional and/or personal needs.

1... You

This is the most important and often overlooked phase of the design process. The people directing the process are the most important determinate to the success of the process. The process begins when you have a proper mental attitude about the project.

This phase provides for the self check needed by everyone involved in the project.

2... Purpose

In this phase of the process, the client clearly defines the purpose of the project (other terms for "purpose" might include the "goal", the "concept", or the "problem statement").

Without a purpose, there is no reason to begin the design process.

3... Situation

In this phase, both the client and the designer each contribute to the development of database that accurately describes the existing situation.

The client provides data describing the number of employees, the communication networks, etc.

The designer provides data describing design considerations which might include code restrictions, etc.

In its broadest sense, the context is the universe in which we live.

The universe is multi-layered, constantly changing, interconnected, and a very powerful constant influence in our lives.

4... Solution

This phase of the process is done by the client, NOT by the designer. It is the time for describing the equipment, organization and image requirements for the design.

This is creative problem-solving on the client's side.

5... Design

The design phase is done by the designers. It involves translating the solution as defined by the client into a physical entity.

6... Evaluation

The evaluation phase is a phase that is also often overlooked. It addresses the question: "Have we achieved our purpose?"

To this point in time, this phase has often been applied in the design of mass-produced items and less often applied to the design of architecture and interior space design.

When you complete this last phase, you will undoubtedly see other opportunities to improve your environment. You will recognize that you are beginning a new cycle.

This is an unending process.

If you wish to visualize the process as a matrix, it would look like TABLE 1:

TABLE 1 The Design Process Matrix

	Gather relevant data	Organize & synthesize the data	Test & validate the conclusion
1 . . You			
2. . Purpose			
3. . Situation			
4. . Solution			
5 . . Design			
6 . . Evaluation			

If you prefer to visualize the process as a flowchart, it would look like this:

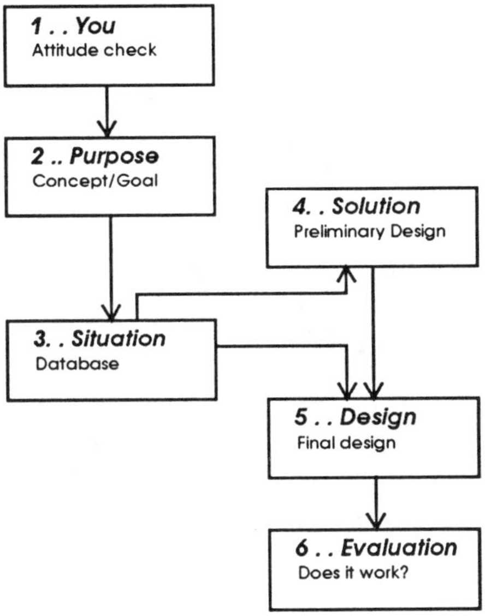

Summary:

This process is very straightforward. You begin by checking your motives for doing the project. You then define the purpose that you would like to accomplish. Next, you describe the existing situation and store the information in a database. You then develop a solution that will accomplish your purpose. Finally, you develop a design that will implement your solution, and you evaluate the result.

CHAPTER 2 ←↑↓→ Gather relevant data

THE PURPOSE

The techniques for gathering relevant data that are described in this section are very helpful for solving design problems but are not limited to the design problem-solving process. They can be used by anyone and applied to any data gathering project.

I cannot over-emphasize the importance of the data-gathering skills. The success of any project is based on a foundation of relevant and accurate data.

Data gathering is one of the first things I look at when I'm working with a situation and can't make a decision. Usually, it simply means I don't have enough information. I enjoy data gathering. I visualize myself as an insect at the tap root of a large tree. I can't see the tree because I'm too small. My challenge is to travel up and down the tree, collecting information as I go. I'm looking to describe the number of leaves it has, the number and relation of the branches, the age of the tree, and even discover what has happened to the tree from the time it was a seed. One piece of information will lead to more questions and more questions lead to more information. The more I look, the more I find. Some of the things I learn will be helpful to me later. For now I'm just enjoying the discoveries. For you, this data gathering should also be enjoyable, but don't let it be the entire focus of the project -- it is only one step in the problem-solving process.

Data gathering, especially in our data-rich age, is not an end in itself, and should be undertaken only after you have established a clear vision of what is wanted and why change is wanted and/or necessary. Then you are ready to gather data to define the present situation, its components (how the system works), why the desired result is not now being reached, and possible options (pathways) for reaching the desired result.

Right answers come from right questions

Everyone agrees that right answers usually come from accurate and complete data and wrong conclusions are often drawn from inaccurate and/or incomplete data.

I have never met a person who made bad decisions, but I have met many people who have made poor decisions on poor and incomplete data. I was working with NASA when the Apollo astronauts died on the launch pad. Do you think the NASA engineers would have made changes in the launch plan if they had more complete information about what was about to happen?

Accurate and complete answers come from asking the right questions. That's why Albert Einstein once said that the questions are more important than the answers. These questions may be logical, emotional, and/or intuitive in nature. Strive to be skilled at asking the critical question. One right question is usually all it takes to identify the critical components. Asking the critical questions is one of the most efficient ways to get the job done.

What you see is the result

When I see an employee whose productivity is low I remind myself that what I am looking at is the result of something that isn't visible. What I see is the result; it is very seldom the problem. The cause is usually much deeper. It may be that the employee is working with faulty equipment or maybe the employee is having problems at home that are occupying his thoughts.

What I see is the best that the employee is able to present, given the circumstances he's working with. I think of what I see as the employee's present form of "damage control."

Quantity before quality

Gathering data is a highly creative skill requiring logic, emotion, and freedom. Although the purpose is stated as gathering only relevant data, (no more and no less than is needed) it is very important not to judge too early what is relevant and what is not. A piece of data that you find may not be helpful when you find it, but it may prove to be very helpful at a later date when it is combined with another piece of data. So don't be too critical at this point.

Quantity increases the likelihood of quality. Later in this process, you will be searching for the controlling issues. Think about this like mining for the diamond: The more dirt you have, the greater the likelihood that it will include the diamond you're looking for. It may be a diamond "in the rough," or it may already be "polished."

The purpose for gathering data is to increase my chances of success by increasing my database of knowledge. I am always amazed at the decisions we make based on almost no information. When you took your last job, did you really know what was involved? Did you research the company? Sad to say, if you're like most people, you made the decision based more on hope or desperation than on information.

Options reduce stress

A problem can be defined as something that you would like to change. Problem-solving involves providing options. Without options, there are no decisions. You simply have to live with what you have. A problem is having a broken arm and not knowing what to do. Recognizing that you have access to a ready-care facility, a hospital, or a clinic immediately reduces your stress level, by providing you with options.

Without options, there are no opportunities for decision making. With options, you have hope and stress is immediately reduced. You can see the "light at the end of the tunnel."

Apply three modes of thinking

I find myself applying three modes of thinking when I'm gathering data. I use logic, I use my emotions, and I use my intuition. Each mode of thinking will provide additional information.

Developing designs

Designs are developed in two ways. Some designs begin with a concept. Data is then gathered and the solution is made to fit the concept. Other designers build from the data. The results are substantially different. The designer who begins with data will gather and organize the data until everything is included in the design.

Designs that begin with concept are often more dramatic and innovative, but seldom work satisfactorily. Designs that derive from data often function but lack the emotional component. The best approach is to combine the two methods, if at all possible.

Recognize assumptions

You will expand your data when you recognize that you are making assumptions and question them. For example: If I assume the problem I'm working with is a design problem and not a management problem, I may not question whether a management problem exists. On the other hand, if I recognize that I have made that assumption, I will go back and gather information about the management of the company. Be aware that you are always making assumptions. Ask yourself:

1. What is known? (facts)
2. What is unclear?
3. What is assumed? (We tend to make assumptions about what is unclear to us)

THE TECHNIQUES

Begin this process by determining to find right data. That may sound strange, but problem solvers will tell you that determination makes the pieces seem to come to you. When people see that you are serious they become serious and pitch in to help. If they think you're not serious, they won't take it seriously either. Once you have made the decision to do an excellent job, the rest of the process becomes much easier.

Keep searching

Without new data, there is likely to be no new insight. Remember that if you continue to do what you are doing, you will continue to have what you have. You need to make some changes. The changes will begin with new information. Determine to keep probing until the new information or the direction presents itself.

Don't be intimidated by dead-ends. Dead-ends are not bad. Rather, they are a useful means for redirecting us. They tell us to go back and re-work our approach.

Avoid procrastination

If you have a problem with procrastination, begin the process by using logic as a mechanical, non-threatening method for getting started in your data gathering. Start getting ready to get started. Get file folders, set up your computer, get pencils, etc.

The most difficult part about getting started is to simply get started, so just jump in. Remind yourself that right answers are less important than just starting.

Manage the time

It's easy to get carried away with data gathering. Some people get carried away with it because it's fascinating. Others because it doesn't demand decisions or conclusions. Others because they are afraid of not including enough data and are trying to cover every possible base.

Whatever the reason, recognize that you could go on and on in this mode and still be unable to identify everything that is involved in the problem you are trying to solve.

The first step is to set a time limit for gathering the data you will base the project on and be done with it. Assign a date and a time to be finished.

Identify the parts

Now begin to identify the parts or the components of the situation (What are the components of the system that is now in place?).

Identify the people:
- Who is involved in this situation?
- What do they do?
- What equipment do they need?
- How do they want their workspace organized?
- What image do they want to project?
- Who should I talk to?

Identify the situation:
- What is involved in this situation?
- Identify what this is a part of?
- What facts would I like to or need to know?
- What makes this situation unique?
- What knowledge and skill will I need to be able to understand this situation?

Identify the location of the situation:
- Describe the existing site
- Describe the present work environment
- Describe the present quality of the site
- Where will I find the situation I need to pay attention to?

Identify the time:
- What time period should I pay attention to?

Identify the present economic considerations:
- Initial cost considerations
- Operating cost considerations
- Life cycle cost considerations

Identify relationships

Use an adjacency matrix to understand the people, spaces, and communication relationships. (Refer to Chapter 14 Figure 7 for an example of an adjacency matrix)

Describe the sequence and dynamics

Now consider the events that led to this situation, the dynamics that are maintaining this situation and the impact of the present situation on the future of the organization. Describe the flow of tasks and events. Identify the key decision points and potential bottle necks.

How does this work?
How did that come about?
What was the original system designed to do?
How does that differ from the present need?
What will this be like 5 years from now?
What will this be like after I have solved this situation?
What changes will take place over time?

Identify the emotional factors

Because each situation deals with people, this component cannot be overlooked. People are more likely to act on emotion than they are on logic.

Review the logic steps and record the emotional response to each of the steps.

Determine what each component feels like.
Describe what the dynamics feel like.
Describe the associations that come to your mind as you think about the situation.

Obtain the observation of others

Network with others, and let them help you. Let them provide a distance and unemotional perspective.

The uniqueness factor

Avoid trying to fit the situation into a mold. Acknowledge the uniqueness of the situation. The uniqueness of the situation will require a unique solution.

The data gathering path may be neither logical nor emotional, but follow it anyway.

Allow time for associating

Creative data gathering techniques can be very effective if they are given time. Schedule time to stop and allow the data to come to you and direct you.

Let the data incubate.

Use visualization techniques

Use visualization techniques to see the situation as an image. When the world-class chess players see the chess board, they do not see the individual pieces, they imagine lines of stress. Apply this kind of thinking for finding the holes in your data gathering.

Use mind mapping techniques (Chapter 14 Figure 9) to help you record these lines of stress, patterns, or images.

Use intuition

Use your Intuition (not trying to "figure it out") to direct your attention to problem and solution areas. Many people would describe this approach as moving on a "hunch". Go with it. The more you do it, the better you will become.

I find that when the complexity of the situation overwhelms the mind, the intuition remains undaunted.

Use free association

This could be described as an even less directed approach. Go with whatever comes to your mind.

Talk to the situation

Now this may sound strange, but try it anyway (you will be amazed at how well it works): Approach the situation as you would a person. Talk to the situation. Ask the situation to present you with the information you will need to solve this situation. Don't make demands of the project, but rather ask and wait. Be patient and move on the hunch.

YOU WILL FIND THAT NEW DATA WILL BRING TO LIGHT MORE NEW DATA. MOMENTUM WILL BUILD AS THE PROJECT EVOLVES.

CHAPTER 3

→↓↑← Organize and synthesize the data

THE PURPOSE

The techniques for organizing and synthesizing the data are very helpful for solving design problems, but are not limited to the design problem solving process. They can be used by anyone, and applied to any organizing and synthesizing project. Organizing and synthesizing is one of the first steps toward excellence in problem-solving.

I cannot over-emphasize the importance of the organizing and synthesizing skills. The success of any project will be based on the ability to identify the critical and controlling factors in the project. If the gathering relevant data skill shows me all the possible places I can pour water, the synthesizing skill shows me where the seed should be located.

This is the opposite skill from gathering and expanding the data base. If the skill of gathering relevant data is a skill of expanding by increasing the quantity of the data, then the skill of organizing and synthesizing is the skill of limiting the data base by identifying the relevant quality factors. Here again, you could visualize an insect that happened to land on the leaf of the tree in search of the tree's tap root. You are working to eliminate all irrelevant leaves and branches in your search for the one branch that will lead you to the tap root. I believe this is the "skill of the Nineties". With all the data that is being generated today, there is an urgent need for individuals who can separate the wheat from the chaff and identify the relevant data.

There are several reasons it is desirable and necessary to organize and synthesize. They are as follows:

The time factor

Each problem, by its nature, limits the amount of time we will invest in its solution. The more critically we view the problem, the more time we are willing to invest. We may invest more time in finding a job than we invest in selecting a new pair of pants.

We are limited in the amount of time we have available (we each have only twenty-four hours in the day), and each of us wants to get the most from the time we have. We do that by identifying the critical issues and working from the most critical issues to the least critical issues.

We rely on the fact that research has shown that if we accomplish the top three critical issues on our agenda we will have accomplished eighty percent of the task. Prioritizing your activities is critical.

It's easier working with less data

The skill of synthesizing is used to reduce the data to a manageable size. The more focused you can become, the easier it is to achieve the goal. I remember a student at Michigan State University being interviewed about life on campus. He said he thought Michigan State University was a bad place. The interviewer asked why he said that. The student reported that he was trying to get into the business school and because of the limited enrollment he would probably not be accepted. The interviewer pressed the issue by asking the student why he thought he wouldn't get in. The student said it was his grade point. Now here's the point: It would be very difficult for the student to be accepted into the business school if he sued the university, and it is unlikely that he would have success changing the limited enrollment policy of the business school. His best strategy is to figure out how to improve his grade point. This is an example of an internal problem (one over which the person has some control) being seen as an external one. The more clearly you understand the situation you are looking to change, the better your chances are of changing it.

More to the point, until you can explain the situation in simple terms, you probably don't understand it.

You have a better chance of solving a problem that you understand. Finding the single most important element in the situation can be very critical to your success.

Enter the data into the mind properly

The fact is that our minds are always searching for meaning. It is important that we provide the data in a manner that the mind can organize and synthesize it.

The left brain works by comparing a very small number of data at one time. It can be intimidated easily by information overload and will "shut down."

Volumes of data lead to increase in stress which leads to procrastination or left brain shutdown. Provide the left brain with reduced data, instead.

The right brain works with spatial relationships. The right brain searches for patterns and thrives on minutiae.

Apply three modes of thinking

Because this is the opposite skill from gathering data, you will want to use the same modes of thinking but directed to identifying the controlling factor. Be prepared to use your logic, your emotion, and your intuition.

THE TECHNIQUES

Moving to exactness . . . . it involves risks and oversights . . . . purposed to efficiency

In order to reduce the data, you are looking to identify the single most important and controlling factor in the situation you are looking at by separating the significant factors from the non-significant factors.

I suggest beginning this phase by using logic. I often begin with logic because it's familiar to me. Therefore, it seems easier and helps get me into the process faster.

Using logic, there are only two ways for organizing things: The process of grouping, and the process of sequencing.

Identify the groups

Begin reviewing the various groups of data you identified when you were gathering data.

Ask yourself if the data groups are the best you can identify. Look for REPETITION and or PATTERNS to appear. Think of each group as a filter for sorting the data.

Consider the list of general categories below:

Group data by people
Group data by activities
Group data by relationships
Group data by site data
Group data by environment data
Group data by quality data
Group data by initial costs
Group data by operating costs
Group data by position in life cycle
Group data by past performance
Group data by present performance
Group data by future considerations
Group data by common size
Group data by common purpose
Group data by common characteristics
Group data by proximity
Group data by function
Identify the pattern with visual imaging

Are these the best groupings you are able to identify?

Identify the critical relationships

Review the adjacency chart you developed when you were gathering data and identifying relationships. Identify the critical relationships in order of importance.

What is the most important relationship that needs to be maintained?

Establish the sequence

Return to the groups you just reviewed. Sequence the various groups to establish hierarchy or priority listing.

Use the decision making matrix (Chapter 14 Figure 11) to prioritize and sequence the groups.

Develop a flowchart to identify the critical work flow pattern.

Identify the most critical emotional issue

The power of association is not to be underestimated. Every object can set off an emotional avalanche within the individual as it triggers associations. Some associations will be positive while others will be negative. Some associations will be logical, some emotional, and still others a combination of the two.

You will want to return to the list of emotional factors you identified when you were gathering data. The source of many problems is not logical but emotional.

Use the decision making matrix (Chapter 14 Figure 11) to identify the most critical emotional components of the situation you are looking at.

Find what others identify as most critical

Use your networking skills to identify someone who can review your findings and give you a distant perspective.

Use visualization to identify the critical factor

Visualize the whole organization in motion from a distance. Now visualize it running at three and four times its normal speed.

Allow your right brain to image the spatial relationships. You could visualize lines of communication or patterns or groups. You could imagine the organization in three-dimensional space as a three-dimensional grid or an exploding star.

Use mind mapping techniques (Chapter 14 Figure 9) to help you see relationships.

In your mind you could visit the situation and visualize yourself at different levels in the organization.

The single entity

Because every situation is unique, you would want to invest time understanding the uniqueness of the situation in front of you. If you are willing to investigate far enough, you will find that behind every problem there is a single decision or factor that is controlling the situation.

Finding that single entity will most radically change the outcome of the project.

While designing for the airlines, the designers studied the factors controlling the design of the airline terminals. The most critical factor turned out to be the parking arrangement of the airplanes. If you change the parking arrangement of the airplanes you will most radically change the configuration of the terminal. Consider what it would look like if you parked the airplanes on top of each other!

Intuition is the controlling factor

Become comfortable with making intuitive decisions. Although most people might not admit it, in reality we are always guessing. Search for the method of organization by guessing. Also, educated guesses are much better than blind guesses.

Give yourself time to stop and allow the data to organize itself in your mind. Remain open to the possibilities. Just because you haven't seen something before doesn't mean it's wrong to see it now.

Finally, ask the data to present its structure to your mind.

BEHIND EVERY SITUATION IS A SINGLE CONTROLLING FACTOR

CHAPTER 4 → Test and validate the conclusion

THE PURPOSE

The techniques for testing and validating the conclusion are very helpful to the design problem-solving process, but are not limited to the design problem-solving process. They can be used by anyone and applied to any situation that requires testing and validating.

The importance of this skill should be self-evident. Consider the value in the stock market of being able to identify a stock, project its success, and accurately test and validate your conclusion before purchasing that stock. And then to reap the dividends from your accurate projection.

It should be equally obvious that this skill is better than no test at all, and still less successful than we would like. This should not prevent us from striving for methods of accurately testing and validating our conclusions at each phase in the design process.

Virtually every project experiences additional expense because someone made an inaccurate projection. The inability to demonstrate that what you expect to happen will happen is costly.

Consider the advantages of testing and validating conclusions before proceeding.

A stopping point

Testing and validating provides a stopping place for each phase of the design process.

Here is a typical situation: I am presently working on the design of a product. We have just completed another prototype table. We are dissatisfied with the result of the design phase. Rather than being discouraged and starting all over as some designers might do, we simply return to our statement of solution. Do we still agree with the proposed solution? The answer is "Yes." In that case, we only need to cycle through the design phase again until a satisfactory design has been completed or the production time has arrived. Going back further in the process would be a waste of time and effort.

Reduce the risks

Because we are able to identify problems early, we are able to reduce the risk of costly design errors. This skill provides us with a safety net.

Testing and validating also provides a better understanding of the risks involved in the project we are working on. This makes decision making easier and more accurate.

Confidence

Testing and validating skills provide a sense of mental security and the confidence to proceed and to explore new creative possibilities.

A simulation

Simulation is at the heart of all testing and validation techniques.

THE TECHNIQUES

If we begin with the easiest and the least costly method of simulation, we would begin with our ability to project the outcome in our mind's eye.

Imagination

Begin by imagining yourself watching your design solution functioning as you would like it to.

Standard techniques

Now let's move to some of the accepted techniques for checking out the possibility of your design functioning as you imagine.

Begin by developing drawings to describe the project. These drawings might begin with sketches or doodles and move to technical drawings and working drawings. See if your design can be drawn out.

You might choose to develop your design on a computer using computer-aided design (CAD) techniques which would allow you to visualize the design in three-dimensional space. You could render the design to help visualize the finished design. You could rotate the design in space and view it from any angle. You might use virtual reality techniques to simulate touching the proposed design before you bring it into existence.

You might choose to construct models of your design to help you visualize the finished product.

You might construct a prototype of the new product. A hand-built, full-scale model of your proposed design that you could test before beginning production might be helpful.

Each of these techniques reduces the risk of costly failures.

Research techniques

You might use standard accepted research methods to determine the ability of your design to meet your expectations.

You could develop surveys to query peoples' responses to various aspects of your design.

You might test-market your proposed design. You could do this by producing a small number of designs and having the public test them and give you their reactions.

Present your ideas to your client

This is the time to present your ideas to the client before proceeding. The following are some considerations in preparing a presentation to your client:

You need to make sure everyone knows the purpose of the meeting. The purpose for your presentation is to obtain direction which will help us in the next phase of the process. Many people erroneously think the reason for a presentation is to show the client our ideas. A response of "That's interesting" is not helpful. We are looking for the directive to correct this or that so that we may move onward with the project. Does the decision maker know a decision is expected? Or does he/she think the meeting is only informational. Since a decision is expected, what information must the decision maker need to have in order to go ahead? And does he/she want any information prior to the meeting? If the timing of the decision is critical, it is important the decision maker isn't put into a position of making the decision without the information he/she wants, or he/she feels blindsided, i.e., he/she thinks the meeting is informational while you expect a decision so the project can go ahead.

Here are some of the preliminary steps involved in conducting an effective presentation (in no definite order):

I. Preparation

   a. Review by briefly describing the present circumstances.
   b. Create a statement of the problem as seen by the client.
   c. Create a statement of the problem as seen by you.
   d. Review the solutions you will propose
   e. Identify results you want from the presentation.
   f. Focus on the audience (Particularly the person making the decision. Make sure you know who must give approval/make the decision and who will primarily influence the decision

maker) What must they get out of the presentation to give their approval?

  g. Develop the presentation strategy.
  h. Develop an overall theme.
  i. Have one clear objective.
  j. Have a concise topic statement.
  k. Write the concluding (summary) paragraph of your presentation first (If you want a specific approval for something, ask for it!).
  l. Draft the presentation/sketches/graphics.
  m. Create a mind map to guide your presentation.

II. Arrange the presentation. Consider:

  a. Location, including seating, lighting, number of people, facilities, and equipment.
  b. Length of presentation (how much time do you need? Can the decision maker give you enough time? Get agreement on how much time will be available).
  c. Time of day (try for a time when the client will be fresh).
  d. Specific types of information requested by the decision maker or a preferred format.

III. Make the presentation

The design concept might be presented by setting up a single workstation for approval. Or, we might complete a single space that will be repeated many times in the proposed design.

CHAPTER 5

1 . . . You - checking your attitude

1 . . You
Attitude check

You might be surprised to find a phase of the problem solving process called "You". That's understandable. No one talks about the importance of the person who will be working on the project as being a part of that project. That's because everyone assumes that you are committed to do the work, capable, easy to work with, supportive of the project, honest, that you have proper motives for taking this project, etc. In other words, they assume that you are a perfect person, but are you?

From your own experience, could you agree that the people have been the greatest help and the greatest hindrance to most project's success? If you agree, you owe it to yourself and to everyone else to take a good look at yourself before you accept the responsibility of any project.

It's easier to run with a hundred people than it is to drag one behind you. If you can't agree with the project, don't get started. It will hurt you and everyone else. If you work on a project, it's your responsibility to be a part of the answer and stay a part of the answer, not become part of the problem.

The psychological phases of the project

Typically, I find myself beginning a new project with great enthusiasm, followed by a phase of discouragement (as I realize how much work is going to be involved), which is finally followed by excitement and satisfaction when the project has been successfully completed. It's not the first phase or the last phase that's difficult, it's the middle phase. In order to prepare myself to successfully complete the second phase, where I become discouraged, I constantly check my work and my attitude.

A self-check list

Begin each project by taking the time to study the project and your relationship to it before signing any contracts or making commitments.

The topics that follow represent some important self-checks that have evolved from my experience working as a problem-solving designer:

It's you, not your project

It's very important for you to keep in mind that you are there to solve someone else's problems -- not your own. Your role is that of the coordinator and facilitator. You are the one to provide the distant perspective and help your client translate their solutions into interior space designs if that's what the project requires. That sounds easy, but it's not.

There will be times in the project when the client will make choices contrary to your recommendations. It's even likely that the success of the project will be dependent on your willingness to design something that offends your personal preference. That's the time you need to remind yourself that it's their project -- not yours.

Success comes from helping others. Zig Ziglar, the motivational speaker, has said "You can have anything you want if you are willing to help enough other people get what they want".

Bring a bias to each project

Recognize that you will have an impact on the project outcome. Let me give you an example of the impact a designer can have on the outcome of the project: If you take the time to look at several Frank

Lloyd Wright designs or several Mies van der Rohe designs you will be struck by the fact that Wright designs look like Wright designs and that van der Rohe designs look like van der Rohe designs. You will also find that it's easier to recognize who designed it rather than what the design is. The statement "form follows function" is often used in the design world. It proposes that the form should evolve from the function it needs to carry out. You will find, however, that form more closely follows the designer (the person defining the form or their personal style). You could say "form follows the designer". All this is not to say that the design is always a reflection of the designer; each of us comes to the project with a bias and that bias can affect our interpretation of the problem.

It's easy to interpret the project in light of our own values, rather than the values of the client. This is most often done with pure but misguided motives. I've watched design students select a chair for a client based on initial price. To the student, the initial cost of things is important, and they assume that it is equally important to their client. Their client, on the other hand, may be looking at a return on their investment over the next fifteen years rather than looking at the initial cost of the chair. The result is that the client is disappointed with the student's choice. You need to always be aware that you can make big mistakes when you bring your bias to the situation. For example, I need to remind myself that my natural tendency will be to look at the project from a male, caucasian, middle class, designer's point of view. To be successful I need to recognize my personal bias in order to consciously remove it from the decision making equation. I need to do this to be honest with myself, as well as to be honest with my client. You will need to do this, as well.

Consider the demands and count the cost

The next check to make is to check your ability and your commitment level to completing the project. You would be better off to not begin a project that you are incapable of completing. Every project offers both opportunity and risk. It's important to calculate both. You must be willing to take on projects that involve both risk and advancement, projects that will help your client and at the same time move you closer to your personal goals: A win-win situation. You might ask, "How much of a risk should I take?" If failure of the project will devastate you, then the risk is too high. If the failure of the project would move you a few steps backward, you might want to take on the project. I agree with business people who say that you should risk not more than 10% of what you have.

Check your self image

To thrive in the second phase you need to have a proper perspective of yourself. You need to acknowledge that you are unique and that you have something worth contributing. At the same time, you need to remember that your point of view is only one point of view.

If you become so concerned about what people think of you that you are unwilling to take the risk for fear of looking foolish, you will probably be unwilling to ask the 'seemingly stupid' question that may need to be asked in order to identify the solution to this project. Many innovations or changes began with a seemingly stupid question. Here's an example: Einstein's theory of relativity resulted from Albert Einstein's question concerning what the world would look like if he was a beam of light. That seems like a silly question, but that was the question that initiated Einstein's theories of relativity. He was willing to ask the question, and to invest the time in finding the answers.

I once worked with the chair of the board of a major airline who would always stop before making a decision and say to the presenter, "Let me make sure I understand what you're saying. You are saying..." He would always risk the possibility of appearing foolish for the necessity of clearly understanding what was being proposed. This is a practice I have found to be extremely valuable. There is no such thing as a "dumb question."

Develop a positive attitude

You will need to have and maintain a positive attitude at all times. You need to maintain your patience and your willingness to change as the pieces of the project come together. The moment you become either bored or frustrated with the project, you are no longer able to do your best. Remind yourself that you need to maintain this positive attitude even when everyone around you wants to tell you what doesn't work and why it won't work. If you agree with them, all hope is gone. Focus on the answer when everyone else is focused on the problem. People will say "This can't be done because we don't have the money", or "That won't work because there is no room." Don't let them rain on your parade.

What may be helpful is to set up reminders for yourself of past successes. These reminders may help prevent the problems from discouraging you.

Try to encourage yourself by recognizing that the only reason you were hired is because a problem exists. Problems aren't problems, they are your opportunities for excellence.

Determine to never quit

Each project seems to have those times when it looks like it's impossible to succeed. That's the time I like to recall Winston Churchill. He gave what is probably the shortest and most significant commencement address ever given. This is his address in its entirety: "Never give up! Never give up! Never give up!" That's the directive to you. No matter what it looks like, never give up. The only chance you have to succeed is to persevere. The successful person is often a person who has just gotten up from falling down just one more time than the others. This is the person who doesn't understand the word "quit."

Prepare to stick with the project until it's completed, no matter what. You've made the commitment, given your word, and there is no turning back.

Do what needs to be done

It's easy to get sloppy during a project. It's easy to expect someone else to do the work you don't want to do. Remain committed to never asking someone else to do what you are unwilling to do. To be successful you must be willing and able and do the work others are incapable of and/or unwilling to do. You must be willing to inconvenience yourself for the convience of someone else. Like the convience store, it's convenient for you at the inconvenience of the store. That makes them successful, and it will do the same for you.

Keep your eye focused on the client's needs, rather than on your own.

There is no substitute for experience

Seek out opportunities to constantly improve yourself so that you can more effectively benefit others. Experience is an important teacher. The more experience you can get solving problems the better you will get at it. There is no substitute for experience. Experience is the primary difference between the professional and the non-professional. Have you noticed that the car insurance rates for the sixteen-year-old are one of the highest premium rates today? Why would that be? The sixteen-year-old today is probably sharper physically, mentally, and mechanically. Then why haven't the accident rates and insurance rates for teens gone down? It's because you can't teach experience. You have to acquire it. The reason the professional is better at his job is because he has solved similar problems again and again. There is no substitute, so always look for ways to increase your experience.

Develop an environment for success

I work in an encouraging work environment. I surround myself with positive people. At the same time I watch, read, and listen to encouraging input about others who have been able to succeed in the areas in which I need to succeed. You should do the same.

Always work on improving

Strive to improve yourself so that you are not dependent on a project or company for your security. I remember listening to a chemical engineer who worked for a large company and was talking about a time in his career when he became dissatisfied with his job and began looking for other opportunities. He interviewed with a small company that looked very good and was offered a position. He hesitated. The owner of the small company asked the engineer why he was hesitating; the pay was better, the work was more interesting, and the working conditions were better. The engineer answered that he was concerned about the job security. He felt there was more security working for a large company than for a small one. The owner of the company said to the engineer, "It's time you recognize that the only security you have is in your ability to perform". That's it!

Be a mentor

Check your preparation level by asking, "If I were hiring someone to solve this problem for me, what are the qualities I would want in that person?" That's the kind of person you want to be. Zig Ziglar, the internationally known motivational speaker, recently did a workshop in which he asked the question of the audience, "Describe the perfect boss." The audience generated a list of outstanding qualities, and then he said "Those are exactly the qualities that you need to have".

Strive for excellence, and strive to be the very best you can be. You should consciously strive to produce the best you can produce. Also, consciously strive to be the type of person you would look up to, the kind of person you would want to hire, the kind of person you would want your children to learn from.

Don't compromise your ethics

A final check you need to make is to compare the project demands with your personal code of ethics. Will this project demand a compromise in your code of ethics? I think everyone at some time is faced with the decision of taking a project that appears to have the potential to greatly advance both our income and our career while demanding some kind of compromise in our personal code of ethics. My personal experience is that anything I have compromised to get I have ultimately lost. This is an area where I recommend walking away from a project opportunity.

I have found that people are searching for someone they can trust more than they are looking for a genius who can't be trusted. Your client isn't buying the project -- they are buying you. They are really buying your integrity and trustworthiness.

The satisfaction of success

The third phase of the project involves the satisfaction that comes from success. There is nothing as sweet as the sweetness of success. Build on your successes, and use them as a mental springboard for the next project.

Let's look at how you might apply the skills in this self check phase of the process. When you have completed this phase of the process you should have a better understanding of your purpose for accepting this project.

Gather relevant data

This is the time to apply all your data gathering skills to yourself. Take a good long look at yourself.

Write down the things that comes to your mind as you think about who you are and your purpose for being.

Write out your hopes and dreams.

Now make a list of all that the project offers.

List all of your motives for accepting this assignment.

Organize and synthesize the data

Reviewing your personal goals, values and purposes, identify what you think is your most important purpose in life.

Now write down what you think is the most important purpose for the project you are considering.

Compare the two purposes. Ask yourself "Is this project consistent with my personal and career goals? Does this project move me toward your goals? What is my real motive for accepting this project? Can I complete this project without compromising my ethics, integrity, and belief system?"

SUMMARY STATEMENT

State your single most important purpose for accepting this project.

→ **Test and validate the conclusion**

See if your summary statement is consistent with things you have done in the past and if it is consistent with your investment of time (is this where you would normally spend your time?).

CHAPTER 6

2 . . . The Purpose for the project

2 .. Purpose
Concept/Goal

The design process begins with a statement of the project's purpose. The purpose is the goal, the thing you are attempting to accomplish. Defining the purpose is a way of beginning at the end.

Just as it's impossible to buy an airline ticket without stating where you want to go and when you want to get there, it's impossible to produce a successful design without defining what you want the design to accomplish.

The purpose addresses the question of WHY you are initiating the project. An example of the purpose of the project might be to travel to California in the shortest time possible. Another example of a purpose statement might be to improve the productivity of the office staff.

It's the client's purpose statement

It is the client who needs to develop the statement of purpose just as the passenger needs to decide where they want to go. The design is the vehicle that gets you where you want to go just as the airline does. This is often misunderstood.

The confusion often begins with the statement of purpose. The client thinks that the purpose is to create a design when in fact the design isn't the purpose but the answer to a solution. Here's an example: The purpose for the project is to find a way of being able to carry out daily meetings without interruptions. The solution is to create a small conference room with ten chairs around a table. It should appear to be a business-like setting. The design is the development of a small conference room.

It is common for a designer to be asked to solve a problem without being given a clear statement of the solution he is asked to design. In fact there seems to be some notion that the less you tell the designer the more creative the solution will be. Let me take a moment to point out the error of this approach. Assume you hired me to go to the mall and select a beautiful coat for you. That's all you said. Now let's assume you also go out to the same mall and purchase for yourself a beautiful coat. What do you think the chances are of our selecting the same coat? Very, very, slim. You gave me no clue about what you like or even what size you wear. That's what designers are asked to do every day. If the designer operates on this "shot in the dark" technique, the chances of success are very small.

Few clients know their own purpose

It has always amazed me how few people understand the purpose of their organization or really understand the purpose of their job. Some time ago, I was asked to redesign some government offices. I asked the department head to describe the purpose of his department. To my surprise he said, "I've never thought of it". He thought about the work he had to do and neglected to think about the purpose for doing the work. I've asked supervisors to tell me what kind of equipment they would be needing and how they would want it organized. More than once the response has been, "That's why we are hiring you".

It's foolish for a client to allow a designer to tell them how they should do their work. You know more about your own business than anyone else. The purpose of the designer is to help you translate your solution into a design that will solve your problem.

Many of the problems we encounter are communication problems that occur during a project because the client doesn't understand what they are all about and/or they don't understand what the designer can and cannot do.

Four possible conditions

The client will be working with one of four possible conditions as they develop their purpose statement. First, they may find that they are developing a statement for a problem that doesn't really exist. Someone only thinks a problem exists. This occurs more often than you might expect. The time to bow out of this request is now. Second, they may find that a problem does exist, but the problem they are asked to develop a purpose statement for is the wrong problem. This often happens. This happens to designers when they are hired by a manager to design a more efficient office. After the installation it becomes apparent that the productivity has not increased at all and in fact the real problem was not a design problem but a management or personnel problem. Third, they may find that they have correctly identified the problem, but they have failed to develop an appropriate purpose statement. Finally, they may have the situation of having received the right problem and having developed a successful purpose statement. Look at this as a wonderful challenge. As a designer, you can only proceed once the client has reached this fourth level.

Focus on the purpose not the problem

The client needs to be directed to concentrate their energy on defining the purpose (defining what they want to have happen). Many organizations will invest inordinate amounts of time defining the problem (figuring out what's wrong). I think it's because we are more familiar with pointing out problems than we are in generating solutions. They may think that a problem well-defined will be half-solved, but many times a problem well-defined may tell you nothing about the solution. Work to keep your clients focused on the purpose rather than the problem.

What would perfect be?

The ultimate question is: "What would perfect look like?" This is a question that is easy to ask and will require real soul-searching on the part of the client to answer. This question will help the client clarify their purpose faster than any other question.

Defining purpose takes time

It may take the client longer to define their purpose than it will take you to create the design solution. This is not as surprising as you might expect. It probably takes you more time to decide what car to buy than it takes to actually buy one.

In my experience, the most common problem is that management doesn't want to take the time to clearly understand and define the purpose of the project before proceeding. No matter how long it takes management to define the purpose, wait. It will ultimately result in major time and money savings for the client. Do not proceed with a project without clear statements of purpose and solution. The solution will become the criteria by which the design will be evaluated.

Working with change

The client would want to consider the influence of change as they develop their purpose statement. Time is a major factor in the design process. Time will have elapsed from the time the design process begins to the time the design is implemented. I am presently working on a project that was begun two years ago, and it is likely that it will be another two years before it is implemented. Both the client and I need to be thinking of the world conditions two years from now for the design to be relevant at the time of implementation, to say nothing of the demands placed on it five years from now. You are always dealing with a moving target. The purpose is likely to remain, but the circumstances will have changed by the time the project is implemented. Imagine what things will be like five or ten years from now, and apply that insight to your purpose statement today.

It can be very helpful to see the project as a part of a larger scheme of things. This may be a little unfamiliar to us in Western culture where we have a tendency to want to break things down into their component parts, but in Eastern cultures it would be common practice to ask what about the project of which this project is a part. Seeing the project in the larger scheme of things will help you feel more comfortable with the idea of change.

Initiate change and direct it

The purpose of design is to bring about change. It makes little difference what direction the change takes. If the change is in the right direction you will recognize it and continue in that direction. If not, you will recognize that and will change your direction. You can't steer a parked car. You have to get it moving before you can direct it. Initiate change and then direct it.

What assumptions are you making?

As your clients finalize their purpose statement, ask them to ask themselves, "What assumptions have we made in arriving at this purpose statement?" This is a very critical question. It forces them to question everything they may have taken for granted. This has proven to be a very powerful tool in freeing them from self-imposed and antiquated restrictions.

What new problems will this solution bring?

The last question you must confront your client with is "What will your next purpose be after you have achieved the current purpose?" This reminds them that design is a process, not an event. The solutions they struggle with today will be followed by others tomorrow.

Note:
Very often when developing the purpose, people will provide information that could impede the process. This might include some detail that will have to be worked out during the design process. When this happens, I recommend receiving the information and immediately recording it in the "Situation" database and move on. This technique proves very effective for keeping people focused on the purpose.

One might apply the skills to defining the purpose of the project as follows:

Gather relevant data

Begin developing your project purpose statement by writing down everything you know about the purpose. The following questions may help you get greater insight.

Even though we are working to generate a quantity of data in the hope that we will have in that data the most important purpose for the project, you will find it useful to include the word "exactly" in the following questions.

IDENTIFY THE PARTS

What exactly is the purpose of this project?

What exactly is involved in achieving the purpose of this project?

Who exactly needs to be involved in order to achieve the purpose of this project?

Where exactly do we need to work to achieve the purpose of this project?

When exactly should we act on achieving the purpose of this project?

If you step back and look at this project as it would appear a year from now how would you describe the purpose of this project?

If you would look at this project from someone else's point of view how would you describe the purpose of this project?

How would others describe the purpose of this project from their point of view?

Gather more information (Talk/read/listen/pray).

Look at the purpose from the opposite point of view.

SEQUENCE

Describe the dynamics of the purpose.

What tasks are you attempting to perform?

Use the question "why?" to get back to the origins.

Organize and synthesize the data

Using the decision chart may prove useful for uncovering the key factor for identifying the purpose.

Decision chart

	Who	What	Dynamic	Pattern	**Total**
Who					
What					
Dynamic					
Pattern					

Statement of Purpose

This is a statement of the single most important purpose for this project.

→ *Test and validate the conclusion*

Is your client confident that this statement of purpose is an accurate statement?

If the test fails, repeat the process until you are satisfied before proceeding.

CHAPTER 7

3 . . . The Situation - describing what you have to work with

3. . Situation
Database

This phase of the problem-solving process involves describing the present situation so that you know what you have to work with.

A central database is established for the project. The client will draw from this database to develop the solution and the designer will draw from the same database to develop the design. Both the client and the designer will contribute to the database.

The client will use the database to describe the number of people involved in the project, the lines of communication that exist, the people problems, the financial concerns, etc.

The designer will use the database to describe the present situation from a design perspective. The designer would describe the present situation in terms of the Function, the Form, the Economy, and the Time. Typical data would include a description of the present site, equipment, furnishings, image, code restrictions etc.

The process of describing the existing situation will itself often provide immediate and obvious clues for developing a solution to achieve the project purpose.

Don't get overwhelmed

Many people get overwhelmed with the process of describing the existing situation. The difficulty is in knowing how much detail to describe. To describe the present situation as "a typical office" is too vague and to describe how many paper clips are in the desk drawer is too detailed.

To get overwhelmed is understandable, especially when you recognize that we live in a closed system where everything effects everything else. Every time you change something in the environment everything else adjusts in response. It's like having a jar of marbles. If you remove a marble from the bottom, all the marbles change their position relative to one another. We recognize that it is impossible to describe how everything is affecting everything else in the situation you are attempting to describe.

Technical intimidation

We can be intimidated by today's technology, which allows us to see more than we have ever seen before and encourages us to gather more and more information. We are tempted to gather more information than we need, and more information than we are able to evaluate. With today's sophisticated databases, it is possible to record the number of paper clips and to reference them in several ways. Computer people seem to thrive on demonstrating the incredible detail which can be manipulated by the computer. This amount of detail can be an encumbrance to the problem solver. It encourages us to miss the forest and see only the trees.

The skill lies in identifying the relevant data and that skill is still based heavily on intuition. Don't underestimate the power of intuition. I've had the privilege of working with some of the finest researchers in the world, and found to my amazement that they spent a good amount of time using intuition and guessing. I would ask, "How did you know that?" and they would say, "I guessed". They told me that the more time they spent using their intuition, the better they got at it.

The rule here is to describe those things that come to your attention.

Don't hesitate to cycle

As you describe the present situation, you will likely find yourself going through the cycle of gathering the data, synthesizing the data, and testing the data several times before you are satisfied that you understand the context well enough to proceed to the next phase of developing the solution. That's normal.

The person is the measuring stick

Don't lose sight of the purpose. Remember that the ultimate purpose for each project is to improve performance of the person. The change in the person will be the criteria for measuring the success of your project.

The designer needs to be reminded that it is not the design that is the ultimate goal or the object to be evaluated. It is the success of the design that brings about the desired changes. Designers, by training, have a tendency to evaluate the design rather than the result.

You may simplify your data collection by concentrating on the data that relates to people.

Working with change

Change is an ever present factor that must be taken into consideration as you are describing the situation.

We need to recognize that the situation we are describing is moving in time. The situation we describe today will be changed when we review our data tomorrow. It is important therefore to describe the dynamics and direction of the present situation.

Can you describe where the present situation will lead if it goes unchecked? Don't predict, just describe the facts.

The environment is constantly moving in the direction of entropy (as it is described by the 2nd law of thermodynamics). It's tendency is to influence both our decisions and our behavior in its direction.

It is useful to stand back from the situation when you look at the change factor. Recognize that you are working with technical change and people change. How much will people change in the next five years? How much will the technology change in the next five years?

Use a check list

A checklist can be very helpful for bringing things to your attention. Use the following sections as a partial checklist for identifying possible areas of critical influence in the present situation. I use these same prompts myself, as I gather the design data relating to projects I am working on.

As you gather this information, recognize both logically and intuitively that it is impossible to gather all the data that might be available. Use your intuition to determine what data are relevant.

The physical, psychological, and spiritual

One way to group the data is to describe the situation as it relates to the physical, the psychological, and the subliminal aspects of the situation.

Realize that these are parts of one continuum, and that they are divided only for convenience. Later you will want to consider the important connections that take place between them.

There are some other things to keep in mind before you begin considering the physical, psychological and subliminal aspects of the situation which I will refer to as the environment:

What you see is the result

What you see is the result of something you don't see. When you have described the situation you will most likely have described a result rather than a problem. The problem is usually not apparent, at least at first glance. Think of the visible situation as a description of the projects' present attempts at damage control.

Refer to the general systems language (Chapter 14 Figure 3). You will see that the results are seen while the causes are often unseen.

The most radical and permanent changes will result when you make change the controlling element in the situation.

The environment is relentless

Finally, recognize that the environment is constantly asking us to do something. It is easier to move with the environment than to work against it. The environment or context can help or hinder us. It can encourage or discourage. It will certainly attempt to influence our decisions and behavior.

THE PHYSICAL ENVIRONMENT

Our body influences and is influenced by the physical environment and our interaction with it.

The physical environment certainly influences our body's ability to function. Dysfunctions in our body will affect our ability to interact with our environment.

We cannot live without this planet's environment. If we destroy the environment, we destroy ourselves. The designs we create are an attempt at maintaining a proper relationship between ourselves and our environment.

The success of the physical environment can be evaluated on two levels. First, we can evaluate the ability of the physical environment to support some of our physical needs, so that we can concentrate on the task we are attempting to perform. On a second level, we can evaluate the ability of the design to enhance our physical capabilities, allowing us to perform tasks better than we could have performed them without the design.

The following is only a random selection of subjects which I use as a checklist to stimulate my thinking as I describe an existing situation. There are many excellent books written on each subject, and I recommend that you seek them out.

ERGONOMICS

This is one of the most talked-about subjects among designers today. It involves establishing an optimum relationship between the body and the equipment with which you work.

It originates from efficiency experts' observation that you could do your work faster if the work came to you, rather than you going to the work. Bringing that concept to reality has resulted in the office today where an individual can sit in a chair the entire workday, without having to move to get the data he needs to do his job.

This has a tremendous impact on the body, and has resulted in the need to design workstations that fit the body better than ever before.

It should not be the purpose of the solution to alleviate the body from having to work, but rather encourage fitness.

TEMPERATURE

Each person has an optimum temperature. One should have reasonable control of the temperature in their personal work space. When the optimum temperature is achieved, temperature will go unnoticed.

WEATHER

The weather influences our body, our emotions, and our attitude. Researches have shown that humidity and barometric pressure changes affect our ability to function. There are optimum weather conditions for each person.

What is referred to as the sick building phenomenon is often found associated with the heating and cooling systems' support of fungus and the like. Allergies are known to be highly influenced by certain levels of humidity.

A body's inability to adjust to changes in barometric pressure can contribute to headaches, and can even result in death. You will find that some buildings today are being pressurized, causing changes in the body as it moves from outdoor to indoor conditions.

LIGHT

The presence or absence of natural light have been shown to influence the body's rhythms. Natural light is known to have a positive effect, while artificial light and it's unnatural rhythm can have an adverse effect on the biological system.

It is known that people respond more favorably to natural light. Many studies have shown that hospital patients whose beds are located near an outside window recover faster than patients who do not have access to a window.

Changes in the body can result from the spectral characteristics, flicker rates, and electrical fields associated with artificial lighting systems. Additionally, our body will make adjustments to compensate for high levels of contrast and/or glare that may be produced by the light within the space. We may tilt our head to avoid glare, and we may find our attention drawn to the points of highest contrast in the space.

Influences of the lighting design have been observed both in the musculo-skeletal system and even at the cellular level.

COLOR

Exposure to the blue portion of the spectrum is known to have a positive effect on removing jaundice from the body. It is accepted as standard protocol in hospitals today to color walls of certain areas blue.

The other portions of the spectrum are likely to affect the body as well.

SOUND

Research has shown that exposure to intense sounds for even short periods of time can be physically damaging to the hearing mechanism.

Studies have also shown that constant sounds over extended periods are eventually blocked out by the body. The body will respond by ignoring or shutting down parts of the system.

Musicians recognize that body functions can be speeded up or slowed down with music. This knowledge is applied in entertainment and in music introduced into the workplace.

SMELL

You may experience allergic reactions to airborne allergins in your environment. These allergins may be emitted from the materials in the area, and may present themselves as odors. In fact, you can be poisoned by toxins in the air. On the other end of the spectrum, the Japanese are experimenting with so-called "aromacology" or "aromatherapy" (the use of scents to stimulate performance, encourage alertness, and/or alleviate stress). Aroma has long been used in marketing and merchandising.

TOUCH

Touch "coding" in everything from water faucet handles to braille writing is used to direct individuals. On the other hand, there are toxic materials that are known to have a negative effect when they come in contact with your body. For example, lead in paint can contribute to lead poisoning.

ELECTRICAL FIELDS

The language of the electromagnetic spectrum, quantum physics, and chaos may become the common languages for describing the complex interaction between the individual and the environment.

We live in an 200-volt electrical field, and our bodies respond favorably to the negative ions within that field. Throughout history, designers have intuitively included waterfalls, fountains, and fireplaces in their designs. Only recently have we come to realize that it is the negative ions present in the waterfalls, ocean spray, fountains, showers, etc. to which we are really responding.

We also respond to other invisible, inaudible fields that can be monitored by EEG, EKG, and other receiving devices. Our body is a composite of interacting rhythms. Each rhythm, when plotted, demonstrates a sine wave. Complimentary rhythms will amplify the wave. If your field pattern matches that of the environment, you will feel the amplification of the wave and report feeling good. Some people might describe this as the type of physical and emotional release they experience when they are in the presence of something beautiful. One could also describe this response as the result of sympathetic rhythms that may occur between the person and their environment.

A final consideration is the phenomenon called entrainment which is the ability of one rhythm to influence another. This phenomenon would suggest that it is easier for your body to comply with the environmental demands than to take a direction on its own. We could simply say that there is the tendency of the body to become like its environment. Since that is the case, it is important to check the quality of the environment we are choosing to spend time in. Choose an environment that will be the most complementary to you and your goals.

The wave patterns called electrical fields are powerful unifying forces in our environment and in our body. We respond to our biorhythms and electrical field fluctuations, with changes in our levels of performance.

These electrical fields can damage or cure. It all depends on how we choose to use them.

MAGNETIC FIELDS

The effects of magnetic fields on living systems are also known. Research has shown that extended exposure to the south pole of the magnet field contributes to aggressiveness while extended exposure to the north pole of the magnetic field contributes to calmness. Notice that many of the most recent medical treatments include the use of magnetic fields.

The new frontier in both health care and environmental design lies in the area of electrical and magnetic field influences on the body.

THE PSYCHOLOGICAL ENVIRONMENT

The psychological environment is every bit as real as the physical environment.

Most decisions are based on what we see

Researchers tell us that as much as ninety percent of our decisions are based on what we see or think we see. The context we see things in can greatly influence our decisions about reality.

Without an environment (context) there is no perception. From all the psychological studies on perception we know that without an ability to distinguish between the environment (context) and the object we are looking at, there is no perception. Further, if you create an illusion by presenting visual information in a manner that violates the operation of the visual system, it will give you a wrong answer. Also, if the eye of the viewer is dysfunctional, you will make incorrect decisions.

You can recognize the psychological environment by asking yourself how you feel in the space you are in. You might find that it feels cold, intimidating, inviting, etc. You might be able to identify some objects that you find yourself drawn to or disturbed by.

The psychological context influences behavior

The power of the psychological environment can be demonstrated by the fact that you probably wouldn't undress in a church sanctuary during a service and at the same time wouldn't hesitate to undress in the examination room of a physician you have never met. The only difference is a change in the psychological associations you have with the one space/function over the other. This response has been learned.

You usually see what you are taught to see

You will most often see what you have been taught to see. In fact there are only two ways to understand a design. Either someone teaches you what the design is supposed to mean or you will apply an association you have with a similar design. Both of those methods are learned responses.

Your psychological interpretation and response to a design may reflect your cultural background. This is why different cultures tend to look at things from different perspectives. Western cultures will tend to divide things into smaller parts while eastern cultures will tend to look at the same thing as a part of something larger. What appears as an illusion to one culture may not be seen as an illusion in another culture.

Each profession will describe the same phenomena differently because their points of view are different. This is a function of their attitude.

You will most often see what you expect to see and you will have the tendency to overlook what you consider unimportant.

Your mind is always searching for direction

Your mind is always searching for the truth. It becomes confused when you present it with two truths. This is the basis for visual illusions and the basis for confusion.

Choose designs that give direction and allow for clear choices.

You describe the world in relation to yourself

You describe everything in your environment in relationship to yourself. This thing is big because it's big in relation to me. This thing is important because it is important to me. I'm important in relation to that thing, etc.

The way you describe the world is highly influenced by your self image and your self image is affected by the way you measure and relate to your environment.

You are always expressing yourself

We cannot help surrounding ourselves with design objects. The objects we choose and the value we give to them reveal to ourselves and others our understanding of ourselves and the world around us.

Your space is an outward expression of what is inside you.

THE CONNECTION

Earlier in this section it was pointed out that everything affects everything else. What you see is simply the result of the things you don't see. It's a continuum.

It may be impossible to say where your mind ends and your body begins. It may be impossible to say where your body ends and the environment begins. That is simply dependent on how you choose to describe it.

We are aware that our body size and uniqueness influence how we think about ourselves.

This body-mind continuum is obvious when we visit a friend who has the flu. Not only is their body affected, but their mind is affected as well. The body affects the attitude and the attitude affects the body. People who have physical problems often end up with mental problems as well and vice versa. The curative affect of laughter is well documented.

RSI (repetitive stress syndrome) is the result of both physical and mental stress. It requires both.

THE SUBLIMINAL ENVIRONMENT

I suggest that the terms "unconscious", "vital life force", and "spirit" can be used interchangeably.

Subliminals are sub-threshold triggers in your environment that affect you on the unconscious level. Subliminals are intended to bypass the conscious screening mechanism and move directly to the unconscious level.

Subliminals may be presented in the form of embedded visuals found in some forms of advertising and/or embedded audible messages found in music. Subliminal messages have been embedded in music played in department stores to successfully discourage shoplifting, and are used in motivational audio tapes as well. The environment itself can be thought of as a subliminal, in that both images and sounds in your environment can affect you without a conscious decision on your part.

The visible environment represents only a very small portion of what is going on in the total environment.

You might begin applying the skills to describing the present situation as follows:

↑←→↓ Gather relevant data

Review the data gathering skills described in Chapter 2, and use them to describe the existing situation from both the client's perspective and the design perspective by describing the various parts that make up the situation, and then describing the dynamic relationship of the parts.

Parts

Begin by reviewing any documents that may be available. This may represent the most solid data available. Then begin gathering additional information by interviewing the key people. Finally, record your personal observations. Review the information in light of the checklist, and record those things that come to your attention.

Establish the major categories of physical, psychological, and subliminal environments to describe the present situation as described by the client, and use the major categories of function, form, economy, and time to describe the design information.

Consider the information from logical, emotional, and creative points of view.

More situation-specific information can be obtained by addressing the following questions:

1. What forces are molding this situation?

2. Exactly when did events begin to change the situation into what I am now seeing? (A time line is a useful tool.)
3. What is really known about this situation?
4. What is known about the present situation?
5. What is unclear about the present situation?
6. What am I assuming as I describe the present situation?

Be sensitive to the fact that you are looking at the situation from a biased point of view.

The Relationships and the Dynamic

Once you have gathered information about the various parts of the situation begin recording the relationships of the parts.

Adjacency charting and mind mapping techniques described in Chapter 14 can be very helpful to identifying loopholes or errors in your data.

Look at the dynamics of the situation. Find out what has changed to cause this present situation to come to your attention? The key word here is change. Flowcharting techniques described in Chapter 14 may be helpful.

Remember that the natural dynamic of the system is toward entropy.

Organize and synthesize the data

Review the techniques described in Chapter 3 for organizing and prioritizing the data.

Look for various methods for simplifying the data. You might see useful patterns emerge, or you might be able to prioritize the data to simplify access.

Try different languages to describe the situation. Flowcharting will provide one emphasis while spreadsheets provide another. Statistical analysis will provide still another point of view. Each language will be useful.

A statement of condition

Because this is a database, a summary statement is not appropriate. It may be helpful, however, to highlight the most critical factors in your database.

Test and validate the conclusion

You can get a feel for the quality of your database by attempting to retrieve various data that comes to mind. Does the database provide an answer to every question you ask? For example, if you ask the database for the number of employees, does it return the number to you, and is the number correct as you originally entered it?

CHAPTER 8

4 . . . Solution - developing the action plan

4. . Solution
Preliminary Design

In this phase of the project you will address the question of HOW you might satisfy the purpose statement you developed in Chapter 6.

Examples of solution statements

In Chapter 6 I gave an example of a purpose statement as: "to travel to California in the shortest time possible". This purpose statement addresses the question of WHY you are doing the project. Buying an airline ticket is a solution that addresses the issue of HOW you might satisfy the purpose statement.

Let's look at the second example from the same chapter. The purpose of the project is: "to improve the productivity of the office staff". The purpose statement addresses the question of WHY you are doing the project. Here are two examples of solution statements that address the issue of HOW you might satisfy the purpose statement: First, develop an incentive program that will provide increased pay consistent with an increase in productivity. Second, redesign the office space to make the arrangement of the office consistent with the paper flow.

Either of these two solutions could satisfy the purpose of improving the productivity of the office staff. The first solution will not require physical changes where the second solution will.

Is it really a design solution?

Is the first solution a design solution? Yes! Design is the process of providing organization and meaning to a situation. It begins with a purpose and it produces a (design) tool. This first solution does exactly that. You begin with the purpose of improving productivity and you produce programs and documents. That's why this book can be helpful to everyone.

What about the second solution? Notice that the second design solution not only tells you what to do, it also gives a broad directive on how it is to be done.

The client provides the solution

Notice that in this process the client is determining the purpose of the project and the solution. You might wonder where the design comes in. The next phase of the process (Phase 5, Chapter) will address WHAT the solution should look like.

Who better to determine the solution to the problem than the person who understands the inner workings of the organization? (This does not preclude bringing in a business consultant to provide a distant perspective to the project.)

The solution is the criteria for the design

The solution statement will become the criteria by which the design will be evaluated.

In the last chapter I pointed out that the way we understand what a design means is to be taught what it means. If you don't tell me what it is supposed to mean, I will apply meaning to the design based on my past experience.

The solution statement serves the function of establishing a common understanding for both the client and the designer. Without this statement the client will evaluate the design based on their personal experience rather than evaluating the design's ability to satisfy the solution statement.

Every designer has experienced the frustration of having their presentation end up in a big discussion of who likes what and why they don't like it. The client always presses to see the design before they have clarified what the design is supposed to do. Avoid falling into this trap.

Developing the solution statement will help both the client and the designer remain focused, and it will clearly describe the criteria by which the design is to be evaluated.

Seek solutions

Focus on solutions. Problems will present themselves. If you focus on solutions the problems become only a change of routing on your journey to the solution.

Describe the image

If the solution that is selected will require the design of facilities, the client would want to include in their solution statement: what they want to have happen, how they want it to happen, and what image they want to project.

Here again, many people would say, "I thought that's what the designer is supposed to do". Notice, I didn't say to describe what you want it to look like. I said tell me the image you want to convey. I would direct the designer to create a new image (that's a very broad directive), or create a high-tech image, or create an informal atmosphere.

Here's another example of image and philosophy. IBM is very proud of it's business efficiency image. Hewlett Packard computer corporation is proud of it's more "casual" approach to getting things done. One is not necessarily better than the other -- they are just different. You would recognize a substantial difference between the two companies just in reviewing the two companies' facilities.

Define the image, and let the designer determine what it should look like.

Address the emotional component

Almost without exception, every project that you work on will involve people. When people are involved, emotions are involved.

Every good salesperson will tell you that there is that moment of temporary insanity when the client chooses to buy the product! Decisions are much more often based on emotion than on logic.

You address the emotional component by addressing what it will **do** more than what it **is**. It's been said, "you sell the sizzle, not the steak". This applies to selling solutions as well.

Support the performers

From experience we know that you cannot use design to motivate an unmotivated employee. Design can be used, however, to greatly enhance the productivity of a properly motivated employee.

The only productive part of any organization is it's productive people. Recognize that they are performers by choice. Support the performers. It is possible that a non-performer will choose to join them.

What you don't want

A method for allowing the problem solver the greatest amount of latitude while maintaining direction and control is to simply describe the boundaries of the problem, or what you don't want to happen.

The purpose statement is "to travel to California in the shortest time possible". The solution statement is "to avoid air travel". That means that you could have the person travel by car, by overnight bus or even on a freight train. Any way you do it is acceptable, as long as you avoid air travel.

Work from the purpose and the situation

You develop your solution statement by first getting your directive from the statement for the purpose of the project and then going into the situation database to find out what you have to work with.

You will want to use the database as an influence and not a directive.

Purge the existing situation

One of the most powerful techniques for solution finding is to purge the existing situation.

Get rid of everything you don't need to make room for what you do need. In a typical office situation employees are responsible for approximately twenty-one linear feet of file storage of which they use one and one half feet. That means that they are taking up thirteen times more file space than they need to! That's space that could be put to much better use. It is also space that is unavailable as long as the dead files are there. Find out what you really need to do your business, and get rid of the rest

This is similar to repairing an automobile that's been in an accident. You need to keep getting rid of the bad parts to find a foundation from which you can build.

This technique has proved to be a wonderful stress reliever and a method for conveying to the staff that something is about to change in their work environment. It's a real motivator.

Starve the problem

An extraordinarily successful solution is to create a situation where the problem cannot survive. You don't address the problem. You address the factors that allow the problem to exist.

In all my years of teaching, I have never had a student come to class in their pajamas. The context discourages it. The problem has nothing to feed on.

Develop solutions that feed or encourage the behaviors you want to have happen and discourage or starve the behaviors you don't want.

Data can provide a logical solution

The data you gather in describing the existing situation will often present you with solutions as you gather the data.

Be skeptical of easy and obvious solutions. Problem solvers refer to these as first-generation solutions. They are important to record, but seldom provide the solution you are looking for. It is more likely that the solution would be some combination of first-generation solutions or something much less obvious.

Developing logical solutions

A wonderful technique for generating solutions is to commit seven days to generating solutions. On each of the seven days, you write out the project purpose and list twenty solutions before you leave your desk or move on to another task. The second day you repeat the same process, making certain that you do not repeat an idea you listed previously. You repeat the process for the seven days.

You will find that the first day is difficult, the second day is more difficult and then as the process becomes easier the ideas begin to flow. It becomes a very freeing process. By the seventh day, you will have a substantial number of solutions.

Creative solutions

When people talk about design, they often think about creativity. Now, you may not think of yourself as being able to be creative, but you are.

Creativity is simply the ability to put two things together that were not together before. It's the ability to see something from a new point of view. Anybody can do it. Designers do it all the time. There are several techniques for enhancing your creativity, which follow:

Encouraging new associations

One way of encouraging new associations is to put yourself in a stimulus-rich environment. Surround yourself with visuals and sounds. Designers will hang drawings all over their work space. They are encouraging their mind to put two drawing parts together on a subconscious level. The result may be a new association or point of view.

Right brain thinking

We should take a moment here to talk about the two hemispheres of your brain and how they affect your logical and creative thinking.

In general, the left hemisphere of your brain is used to process logical information. This is the hemisphere that we have educated and the hemisphere that we use the most. This hemisphere wants to process information in a sequential order.

The right hemisphere of the brain processes information spatially and in images. It tends toward free associating and the reduction of complex data into whole pictures. It is this hemisphere that we want to activate to create new associations.

To activate the right hemisphere of your brain you need to turn off the left hemisphere. It's as if the right brain is hidden by the left. To shut off the left hemisphere, we can present it with information more complex than it wants to handle, or present it with no information at all. In both instances, the left hemisphere just shuts down.

Although you may not realize it, this is not a new experience for you. You already drive your car more often with the right hemisphere than with the left. You don't consciously consider all the logical decisions that need to be made, you just drive. It works because the left hemisphere doesn't want to deal with all the possibilities.

When you place yourself in such a stimulus-rich environment, the left hemisphere tends to shut down and the right hemisphere goes to work putting pieces together.

Free association

One might also consider free association, the process of writing down the random thoughts that come into your mind and attempting to associate those thoughts with the purpose you are trying to solve.

Forcing new associations

A more direct approach is to force associations. Designers may begin by identifying the various parts of a design. Let's use a highlighter pen as an example. They would make each part of the pen the heading of a column. One column would be titled "shape", another "cap", another "cartridge", etc.

Then they would list in each column some possible alternatives. Shapes could include a sphere, a cylinder, a cube, a cone, etc. Cartridges could be modular, built-in, replaceable, etc. This process is applied to each column.

When you have filled in this chart, randomly select one characteristic from each column and assemble them into an image of a possible highlighter. For example, you could imagine a highlighter that is in the shape of a cone, without a cap, that has a replacable cartridge.

The number of possible forced combinations are almost endless. You could apply the same process to a room. You would identify the parts: The ceiling, the floor, the walls, the door, etc. You would identify alternatives for each part and then, selecting one alternative for each part, you would assemble an image of the room.

The purpose of this exercise is not to happen on the right solutions as much as it is to expand our thinking.

Involve others

Involving others will help you generate new perspectives. There is great value in networking with others. Very often, someone else will see an "obvious" solution that you were unable to see yourself.

What does perfect look like?

Instead of attempting to solve the project by developing solutions, stop and identify what the perfect solution would look like. Work backwards.

Changing the language

Another method for generating new insight is to describe the situation using several languages. Each time you change the language you will find that you have gained new insight. Describe the situations verbally, then try to draw a solution, or try to build a model of the solution. Try using a mathematical formula to describe the situation, or try relating the solution to music.

Different languages often cause different thinking strategies.

Ask for the impossible

Asking for the impossible is a wonderful technique for breaking the logic barrier. Again, the left brain will shut down at this kind of proposal and you will be forced into creative solutions.

This works time and again. Take whatever problem you are working on and make it ten times more difficult. For example, if you are having difficulty adding one more file cabinet in your office, think of what you would do to fit ten file cabinets into your office.

Generations of solutions

This is the process of combining more than one solution to form another solution. We refer to the first ideas as first-generation ideas. We then describe combining two first-generation ideas to form a second-generation set of ideas.

You can also create third- and fourth-generation solutions using this process, to further expand your pool of possible solutions.

Solutions after next

Activate "forward thinking" or anticipating by asking, "After we have solved this problem, what will the next problem look like and what will be the solution to that problem?" Each solution will contain the seeds of the next set of questions.

Be prepared for anything

Be prepared for anything. As a designer, don't be concerned if your best solution doesn't involve designing a facility at all.

Don't be intimidated when your best solution doesn't look like anything you have seen before. It's not wrong just because you have never seen it before.

Avoiding criticism

In the beginning of the process, it's very important to avoid criticism, so that mediocre solutions that could lead to better solutions are not discarded.

It's also very helpful to avoid discussions about money early in the process. Budgetary concerns are much easier to deal with later. The task before you is to develop a solution.

As an example, it is far more difficult to develop the concept for the Ferrari than it is to design the Fiero. The challenge is to develop the original concept. It will always be relatively easy to design a cheaper copy.

The value of exact definitions

Tremendous savings can be seen by carefully defining the requirements for the exactness of the project. In general, it is more efficient to design for a more exact specification than it is for a specification that needs to address several issues.

You may be more effective and save substantial costs if you specify a television antenna that will receive only channel eight rather than a television antenna that will receive twenty channels.

At the same time, if you are too specific you defeat your purpose. If, for example, you were to go so far as to specify a certain manufacturer and model number for an antenna that will receive only channel 8, your likelihood is that you will pay more than you need to in order to receive channel 8. Your supplier might be able to get it for you, if it is what you really need or want, but it may be unrealistic and highly cost-ineffective to be this specific.

As a more complex example, Einstein's formula ($E=mc^2$) which applies to all energy/mass, all the time, may be more useful than a formula that describes some energy/mass in certain instances.

The design program

The solution statement we have been describing is a part of what the designers refer to as the programming document for the project.

You could apply the sills to this phase as follows:

Gather relevant data

Begin this solution-finding phase by returning to the purpose statement and keeping the statement in front of you at all times. In this way, your conscious and unconscious mind is always reminded of the task at hand.

You should then determine the amount of time you have to come up with the solution. It may be easiest to break it up into a cycle consisting of logic analysis, creative exploration, and logical review.

During logical analysis, first, review the situation database. Then, purge (get rid of everything your don't need) the existing situation. After purging the situation, look for the data to present you with logical solutions. Finally, apply the logical based solution-finding techniques.

The second block of time could be used to explore creative solutions. Selecting from the techniques described above, apply as many techniques as you have time for.

It is very important to stay especially alert during this phase of the process and to keep a pencil and paper or a tape recorder near you at all times.

The solution often comes and goes very quickly. We have all experienced having a great idea only to be unable to recall it a minute or two after we had it. I have seen people scribble an idea on their shirt rather than lose it. I know people who keep a paper and pencil at the side of their bed.

Organize and synthesize the data

I usually use a decision chart (see example, Chapter 14 Figure 11) to help me compare each solution with every other solution and rank them in terms of their potential.

I then check to see that my solution addresses both the logical and the emotional components of the purpose statement.

If the best solution requires the design of facilities, I make certain my solution statement directs the designer in terms of the equipment that will be required, the method of organization, and the image I want to convey.

STATEMENT OF SOLUTION/DIAGRAM

This statement describes the solution which will be the criteria for evaluating the success of the project.

Test and validate the conclusion

Is there internal agreement on the solutions statement?

Is this a win-win situation where everyone gets some advantage?

CHAPTER 9

5 . . . The Design - developing the instrument that will implement the solution

5 . . Design
Final/preliminary

In this phase of the project you address the question of WHAT the solution will look like.

Following our example of traveling to California, If the PURPOSE is to travel to California in the shortest time possible, and the SOLUTION is to travel by air, then the DESIGN is the airline that gets you there.

The task of the designer, then, is to create the airline.

Following the example of increasing the productivity of the office staff, if the PURPOSE is to increase the productivity of the office staff, and the SOLUTION is to design the office to reflect the paper flow and present a certain business image, then the DESIGN is the office.

The design is a tool/instrument

You can think of the design as a tool or instrument that has evolved from the solution statement and the situation database.

The design brings about the solution by providing organization and meaning to the situation. The completed design will enhance the performance of the person and reduce stress.

The concentration is on the process

It's common to think that the role of the designer is to develop a design, but in reality the designer concentrates on the design process which in turn produces the design.

The design is the necessary result of this process.

Designing a facility

Let's discuss some major issues that are involved in designing the office facilities we have been discussing.

Our mind is always searching for meaning. Without the ability to bring some organization and meaning to a situation, the mind becomes very confused and will ultimately shut down.

The designer will provide organization to the situation and will assist in assigning meaning to that organization.

The strategy is to work from the very general to the specific. In this instance, you would work from the solution statement to the design details.

The organization

You will find that designers provide organization at various levels. Look at the building you are in right now. You will find that it is related to the buildings around it. The walls of the building you are in are not located randomly, but they are organized. Within the walls, the furniture is organized, and within the furniture the components are organized.

The organizing techniques are the same for the designer as they are for everyone else. They involve organizing things into groups and/or organizing things in some hierarchy or sequence.

Since the solution involves space, the designer will begin by organizing things on flat surfaces (like floors). Then the designer will consider utilizing three-dimensional space and cubic space (utilizing wall space and ceiling space), and finally the designer will consider the elements of sequence and time.

Fit

The designer is organizing the elements to fit the existing solution, the existing space, the people, etc.
The design should be thought of as an extension of a person. It needs to fit like an old pair of shoes. It shouldn't cause blisters (However, even the very best designs still need to be "broken in").

Many people have never experienced what proper fit feels like. If you would take you pants off and put them on backwards you would find that it's a very uncomfortable experience. However, if your mother always dressed you with your pants backwards, you would think that's the way it was supposed to feel. You might continue that way without ever giving it a second thought. I think that we experience and accept that kind of design misfit in many areas.

The ergonomic office chair can be used to illustrate this point. The plastic shell chairs that we thought fit well a few years ago are no longer acceptable now that we have experienced a properly fitting chair with lumbar support and other enhancements.

Here is what the designer is doing today: The designer will work at organizing the situation until the user can grasp the organization and get a sense of place. Then the designer stands back and expects the user to fine-tune and personalize the design for themselves. An example is the design of the grocery store. The designer has controlled the organization of the shelving, the produce area, the meat, and the refrigerated sections. If an employee in the produce area changes the display, it does not destroy the organization of the department or disorient the user.

Unfortunately, many people don't do the fine tuning. It's like a person having a pair of pants with legs that are too long. The pants keep dragging on the floor because they haven't been hemmed to the length they need to be.

Pull, don't push

Designers have better success when they create designs that work to help you rather than to hinder you. In design, as in human motivation, the directive is to encourage rather than to force. Design should encourage the people in the desired direction, not push them.

The meaning

The second responsibility of the designer is to provide meaning.

The results of a design will be greatly enhanced when you take the time to inform the users of the purpose for the change and then backup those changes with the design changes.

When the client develops the solution statement in-house, he is preparing the staff for change. Before the design is even introduced, it has been assigned a meaning. The meaning is the solution statement.

In the office example described earlier, the SOLUTION is to design the office to reflect the paper flow and to present a business-like image. The staff is informed that the company is going to help them improve their work performance by making the office layout consistent with the paper flow. At the same time, the company informs the staff that they are looking to support their staff by providing a better working environment by creating a more business-like image. When the design is presented to the staff, that is what the design will mean to the staff. Each time they see the design they will remember that the company is interested in helping them to improve their performance on the job and in improving the staff's work environment. If, however, the meaning is improperly communicated or is not presented initially, the staff may assign their own meaning, and be critical or resentful of the design changes.

You educate the user by drawing their attention to the solution statement before they see the design. If you don't do this the people will assign their personal meaning. These personal meanings will vary widely.

Here is an example: I have a friend whose son was petrified of fire engines because every time he saw a fire engine stop at a house, there was a fire there. When he heard the sirens, he would invariably start to cry. He was afraid the fire engine was going to stop at his house. He thought that fire engines start fires.

Other people will bring equally unexpected meanings to your design if you fail to present them with the solution statement first, so that they know what the design they are about to see is supposed to mean.

What about beauty

People value things that support them. The first time we see something new, we may not like it, but if it works for us we come to value it and call it beautiful. When a new style of clothing comes on the scene we may be shocked. We may hesitate buying it and hesitate wearing it. People may make a nice comment about how good it looks and soon it's a favorite part of your wardrobe.

The importance of timing

The timing for the introduction of a design change is critical. This is so important it bears repeating.

The time to introduce a design change is when you make a change in business direction. The design then becomes associated with the change. This is especially powerful if the employees are involved in the change process.If you change the business direction without changing the design you will find that the change is far less effective. The reverse is also true. If you make design changes and do not make business changes, the staff brings the same old habits to the new environment and the result is less effective.

The preliminary and final designs

Designers will develop the design in two phases; the first phase is referred to as the "preliminary design phase". In this phase the designers develop drawings and diagrams that present the design in general terms to confirm the validity of their approach.

Designers will generate several preliminary designs before proceeding to the final design. The preliminary design allows for midterm corrections and may even suggest some modification in the proposed solution.

The second phase is referred to as the "final design phase". This phase involves working out the details agreed upon in the preliminary design.

You can apply the skills to developing the design in two sub-phases as follows.

Gather relevant data

PRELIMINARY DESIGN

Get direction from the solution statement

Begin the preliminary design phase by reviewing the solution statement. This statement gives you specific directions on what to do.

Get data from the database

Go to the situation database and begin organizing the various components as directed by the solution statement.

This would include gathering information about the sizes of the components and may even require drawing the components to scale.

Develop block diagrams

Having organized the components into various groups suggested by the solution statement, determine the size of the group in square feet.

Draw to scale a rectangle to represent each of the areas that will make up the design.

Consider several diagrams

Develop several arrangements of the rectangles that could satisfy the directives of the solution statement.

Develop arrangements in both two-dimensional and three-dimensional space. Finally, develop arrangements that take advantage of time. Consider sharing the space with one person using the space at one time and another person using the same space at another time. What you have been drawing are referred to as block diagrams.

From the situation database, obtain a drawing of the space that is available to you (make certain the drawing of the space that is available to you is drawn at the same scale as your block diagram).

Develop a block diagram that will fit the space that is available to you.

Develop the image

Develop preliminary designs representing the image you are proposing.

Present your work to the client for further direction. Many people think the purpose of a presentation is to simply show what you have developed. The purpose of the presentation is to get direction on what to do next. This could be in the form of developing more preliminary designs or asking you to begin developing the final design.

FINAL DESIGN

Design the support systems

Develop the support systems for the design. This would include the mechanical systems, meeting code requirements, etc.

Detail the design

Work out the details of the design.

Specify and oversee the construction

Develop the specifications and the construction drawings. Write the specifications and order the furnishings.

Oversee the construction and assist the client with the move in. Any discrepancies or problems that arise at this point need to be worked out per the original contract drawn up with the client.

Organize and synthesize the data

PRELIMINARY DESIGN

Select the best block diagram

At the end of the preliminary design phase and before presenting your preliminary design to the client, select the best design.

FINAL DESIGN

Select the best contractors

At the end of the design phase, select the best contractors to do the work.

FINAL DESIGN

The final design may be presented in the form of a drawing, a model, a mock-up, a computer image, an animation, or a virtual reality presentation.

Test and validate the conclusion

When the client's response to your design is: "Of course, what took you so long?", you will know you have succeeded. The right answer is always obvious in retrospect.

CHAPTER 10

6 . . . *Evaluation - checking the effectiveness of the design process*

6 . . Evaluation Does it work?

In this phase of the process you will evaluate the ability of the DESIGN to achieve the PURPOSE. The PURPOSE is the criteria by which the design is evaluated. Recognize that in order for the PURPOSE to be achieved, you will need to correctly identify and develop both the SOLUTION and the DESIGN. In our example of traveling to California, the SOLUTION was to travel by air. The EVALUATION addresses the question. "Did you get to California in the shortest possible time?"

In the example of improving staff performance. The PURPOSE was to improve worker performance. The EVALUATION addresses the question. "Does the office design improve the performance of the staff?"

Notice that the travel EVALUATION question does not address the issue of whether traveling by air was the shortest method of getting to California. That was resolved in the selection of the SOLUTION. The office performance EVALUATION question does not address the issue of whether redesigning the office to reflect paper flow and initiating a business image would improve staff performance. That was also resolved in the selection of the SOLUTION.

Two methods of evaluation

There are two methods of evaluation: The logical method for evaluating the design and the emotional method.

These two methods of evaluation will result in different selections. One method of evaluation is not intrinsically any better than the other. They are both useful.

I have often asked my design students to evaluate the projects that were submitted. We develop a logical criteria and give a number value to each area we were going to evaluate. We assign a value for having addressed the clearance requirements, a value for the choice of furnishing, etc. I would then ask each student to evaluate each project.

I would then ask the student to review the same projects one more time and simply identify the project that they liked the most. Almost without exception, the project they liked the most was not the project they gave the highest score.

Think about this example to remind you of the importance of understanding the method of evaluation that will be used to evaluate the success of the project.

Human nature favors the emotional decision. This does not mean that the logical and technical aspects of the project can be ignored. Think of it this way: The decision will likely be based on emotion, and you need to score your work to verify for yourself that you can produce the result you are going to present to the client.

We find ourselves making these emotional decisions so often because it is really impossible, or at least too difficult, to accurately compare any two products anyway.

As an example of this, the next time you walk in the mall, give yourself the challenge of finding the "best buy" on running shoes that day. I'm not talking about simply comparing the price of the same manufacture and model shoe. I'm talking about being able to logically compare one manufacture and model to another. You will quickly find that there are too many variables to compare and that you don't really understand how to compare the value of leather to some other material anyway.

Some problems inherent in evaluating office design solutions include the fact that a long period of time will elapse between the time the solution is proposed and the time the result will be seen. Changes will have occurred, making evaluation difficult. In addition, the uniqueness of each situation makes the technique of learning from others' experiences much more difficult.

It becomes important, then, to recognize that you are making emotional, intuitive decisions. You make your decisions based on trust. You trust your intuition, you trust your emotions, and you trust the people who are helping you make the decision.

Many points of view

In addition to the logical and emotional methods of evaluation, you will want to recognize that each design can be evaluated from several points of view.

I recall making presentations to several senior vice-presidents of an airline. Each person in the meeting was there to evaluate the design from their point of view. One person would represent the passenger services point of view, another would represent the maintenance point of view, another would represent the economic point of view, and so on.

Recognize that each point of view may be in conflict with the others. Although the passenger service person might really like the idea, the maintenance person might think it was awful from a maintenance point of view, and the economics person might think it was too costly.

Every design will address only one issue at a time. When you start with the SOLUTION statement, you have just set a priority to the possible options. If your first decision is that the building is to be the most beautiful building ever designed, then it probably won't be the most inexpensive building.

Who is responsible?

In the same way, you need to identify the most important point of view that will be used to evaluate your design and meet that point of view first. Other points of view will be addressed, but in their order of priority for that project. In addition it is critical to identify the most influential person. This person might not be the person with the positional power, but the person who influences the person with positional power. For example, the executive secretary may influence the office design decision more than the CEO will. Finding out who has the influence may be the real trick.

Another point of view

Another way to look at the value of a design is to ask how many problems the design will solve and how long the solutions will work. I find it useful to locate the value of each project on a matrix. I use one axis of the matrix to describe the number of problems the design will solve in their order of priority and I use the other axis to describe the length of time the solution will be effective.

In general a design solution that does a better job of solving more problems for a longer period of time might be considered better than a design that solves a problem in a very limited situation for a very short period of time.

The following tips may be helpful for applying the skills to this phase of the process.

Gather relevant data

Identify the various points of view

Begin by identifying the various points of view that will be used to evaluate the project.

Organize and synthesize the data

Recognize that the various points of view are in conflict while others complement one another.

Develop a criteria for evaluating the design by prioritizing the points of view.

Use a decision matrix to compare each point of view and identify the most critical point of view.

CRITICAL POINT FOR EVALUATION

State the most critical point of view and be prepared to address that point of view.

→ Test and validate the conclusion

Look at the person, not the design

Does the design bring about positive changes in the person? To bring about a positive change in the person means that the DESIGN has successfully implemented the SOLUTION and that the SOLUTION has successfully achieved the PURPOSE.

The ultimate goal is positive change in the person.

Beauty is learned

We learn to accept change, and we find ourselves caring for the design when it is supporting our needs.

Any design that does not support us will be abandoned, adapted, altered, and/or destroyed, i.e. -- only objects we care about will be maintained by us.

CHAPTER 11

Applying the design process to identify your life's purpose

1.. You... What's your attitude about doing this project?

In this phase of the process you address the issue of WHY you should be personally involved in this project.

You begin this project as you do every project, by checking your attitude, your motives, and your ability to do the work.

This project involves applying the design process (providing organization and meaning) to the design of your life.

If you're not interested in this project, you're bored, you're frustrated, you don't want to take the time, or you're unwilling to accept the demands the project will make of you, you will either need to make the necessary changes or stop right now.

It is counter-productive to everyone involved for you to start something that you won't complete.

You limit the success of the project

Keep in mind that you are critical to the success of this project. Your physical, emotional, and spiritual capabilities will be major factors in reaching the project goals. The solutions you seek will never be better than you are.

Excellence is available to you

Think about how many people have succeeded in living a happy and joyous life. You will find that achieving excellence has little to do with education, intellect, or background. It has everything to do with maximizing what you have to work with.

We could cite example after example of people who had everything going for them and yet failed at life, and at the same time we could find example after example of people with seemingly nothing going for them who succeeded. Some people think that just being in the right place at the right time is the answer, and that's partly true but, the real key lies in the people.

You need a plan

Excellence is the result of planning. Today only five percent of all people have a plan for their life. Some people think that excellence just happens, but this is seldom the case. Excellence is the result of opportunity and preparedness coming together. You must be prepared when the opportunity comes and that takes planning.

Check your attitude

Activity and attitude go together, you don't have one without the other. If you have a positive attitude you will take positive, confident steps toward your goal. Not only that, your enthusiasm will become contagious and others will want to help you.

Check your motives

Check your motives. If this project is directed to helping others succeed, you will succeed. If your motives are only self-centered and self-serving, the project will ultimately fail.

Check your self image

As a person, you have a unique contribution to make, so don't expect it to be just like everyone else's. It may be scary for you to recognize that you are unique until you recognize that everyone else is unique also. Your uniqueness is exceedingly valuable, so accept it.

Check your commitment level

The challenge lies in getting yourself to do what you know has to be done. Commitment demands a quality decision that says: "I will, until it's done". Once you have made that quality decision, everything becomes focused and easier to achieve. It's actually easier to be outstanding than it is to be mediocre.

Take this old saying as your project motto. "If it's going to be, it's up to me". The only way you will get this job done is if you do it. No one has more interest in your success than you do. If you are willing to do the menial things, opportunities for excellence will come your way.

Work on character

You can't be one kind of person and another kind of employee or professional. Work on your character. Character is far more desirable and difficult to come by than technical skills. Show me someone that is interested in the work, trustworthy, teachable, and trainable, and people will help them to achieve success.

You have exactly what you want

Take a good look at yourself. Right now you have exactly what you want. If you didn't want what you now have you would be making different decisions. Your present position is the result of your past actions.

You may find that you will need to develop new skills to complete this project. Changes will require effort but if you continue to do what you are doing, you will continue to have what you have.

Invest in your strengths

Don't get caught up in thinking the grass is greener on the other side of the fence. It's not. Don't waste your time trying to be something that you're not. Invest your time in doing what you're good at. Do more of what you do well, and do it better.

You can change

As long as you have brought your last responsibility to closure, you can change your direction. Never leave a project before it's completed.

The cowards never begin and the weak will drop out along the way.

Gather relevant data

Take a few minutes to jot down some of the emotional, logical, and creative reasons it is to your advantage to become personally involved in this project.

Some of your reasons might include the fact that only you could do the work, it's a challenge, you are working for the payoff, or you see an opportunity to help others.

Use this TABLE to record some of your reasons.

TABLE 1 Some motives for doing this project

	Logical	**Emotional**	**Creative**

Organize and synthesize the data

Now take a moment to look at your list. Use the columns at the right of the table and use a check mark to note whether the motive is Logical, Emotional, or Creative. It could be more than one.

A logical motive might be that you know you will perform better if you do the project. An emotional motive might be that you will feel accomplishment after you complete this type of project. A creative motive might be that you want to see if you could make a game out of your life plan.

Be honest with yourself as you identify your real reason for doing the project. Your motives will usually be obvious to you at this point. You may need to combine two or more statements to make an accurate and complete statement. When you've identified your motives, initial the line below.

I am committed to doing an excellent job!

____

Test and validate the conclusion

Check to see if your reason is consistent with your time commitments.

Keep your motive in front of you at all times. Write it on a card that you can keep in your pocket.

2. ..*Purpose...* What is your life's purpose?

In phase "1" you addressed WHY "*you*" became involved in the project. In this phase you address WHAT the "*purpose*" of your life is all about.

Be clear

The more clearly you can define the purpose of your life, the easier it will be to achieve. This will require making decisions and focusing your attention.

You will find that you can be outstanding in some areas, but not every area. You need to make choices because you are limited in time.

Stay focused

To remain focused on your purpose is critical. It requires commitment.

The big picture

Get a big picture. See how you fit into that purpose. What can you contribute to the world?

Many people think that a project of this type is to find a job, but it's more than that. It's identifying the contribution you can make, identifying the life-style you want to live, identifying the career or profession that will support that life-style. Although your career is not your life, it is a major factor in it.

Planning your life is not being self centered. The better you function, the better you can help others.

It always involves people

Everything goes back to our co-dependency. It is based on the fact that we are more powerful as a team than as individuals. It takes teamwork to get things done today. Could you grow the cotton, weave the fabric, design, and sew together the shirt or blouse you are wearing? Could you have built the computer you are using? Probably not. We are dependent on each other. You are needed. No man or woman is an "I" land.

Attend to others

You must direct your attention outside of yourself. You can have everything you want if you are willing to help enough other people get what they want. The demand is for the person who is willing to give. The system favors the performer, not the rider.

Gather relevant data

To arrive at a statement of the real purpose for the project, you would want to take a few minutes to develop a menu of possible purposes.

You may want to make money, be physically fit, have a family, have friends, and have time to yourself.

1. Use the first section of TABLE 1 to list some of the things that you would like to accomplish.

   It's not so much a time to be practical as it's a time to search within, and to identify what's really in your heart. Search for things that are worthy, that give you a sense of worth, that you could love, and that would allow people to love you for.

   The idea here is to think about your life and its possibilities from as many points of view as you can.

2. Use the second section of TABLE 1 to think about and record the assumptions you had to make in generating your list of things you would like to accomplish.

3. Use the last section of TABLE 1 to think about and record what you would do if you accomplished all the items on your list of things you would like to accomplish.

TABLE 1 List some possible purposes

	Logic	Emotion	Creative
List some things you would like to accomplish			
List the assumptions you are making			
List your purposes after these have been accomplished			

Organize and synthesize the data

The purpose for organizing and synthesizing TABLE 1 is to attempt to identify your single most important purpose in life.

As you develop this statement of purpose, you will find that some detail, important to the project, but distracting to the concept, will come to mind. It might be remembering that you need to schedule a dental appointment, for example.

To avoid losing any significant details and avoid being distracted from identifying the real purpose of the project, write down every significant detail that comes to you. Later you can locate it in the database you will be developing in the "Situation" phase of the process.

1. You can begin to reduce the many purposes you listed in TABLE1 to a single most important purpose by putting a check in the appropriate box indicating whether there is a logical, emotional or creative conclusion.
2. Look at each of the logical responses you put down and rank them. Put an "H" by the high priority, "M" for moderate priority, and "L" for the low priority.
3. Now go back and rank the "H" priorities numerically. Give the highest priority 1, the second 2, the third 3, etc. Place the appropriate number after each letter. Your entry might look like "H1" or 'M3".
4. Repeat the process for the emotional responses and the creative responses.
5. Develop a statement that describes what you want to have happen. This purpose statement is your mission statement or your goal statement. While many people concentrate on defining the problem, you concentrate on the purpose. That will lead you to the answer.
6. Write the statement down.

My single most important purpose is:

____

This is the thing that you most want to accomplish.

You would want this purpose to include:

a. something of worth.
b. something worthy of your commitment.
c. something that allows you to be loved.
d. something that gives you a sense of accomplishment.

→ *Test and validate the conclusion*

Take time to really think about your purpose statement and:

1. Check to see if your statement is consistent with your inner FEELINGS.
2. Check the statement against your ACTIONS. You invest your time in direct proportion to your priorities.
3. When you are comfortable with your statement, move on to the next phase.
4. Give your summary statement to at least 5 people and ask them to tell you what they think it means. When they give you the answer you expect, you'll know your summary statement is clear.

3 . . . *Situation* . . What do you have to work with?

In this phase you will want to assemble a database of information about yourself.

Gather relevant data

A time to take inventory

This exercise is an exercise you can use any time you want to quickly give yourself a checkup.

1. Begin with an exercise called "The wheel of success". (See TABLE 2)
   a. Think about the graphic in table 2 as a wheel with seven spokes. Consider the center of the wheel to be "0" and the rim to be a "5".
   b. Look at each spoke and describe your present level of success in that area by putting a dot along the spoke to represent your level of success. If you were dead you would put the dot on the spoke at the center "0". If you have achieved total success, put the dot on the rim "5". Now, if you are some place in between, as you should be, put the dot in the appropriate location from "1" to "5".
   c. Repeat the process for each spoke.
   d. Connect the dots.

TABLE 2 The wheel of success

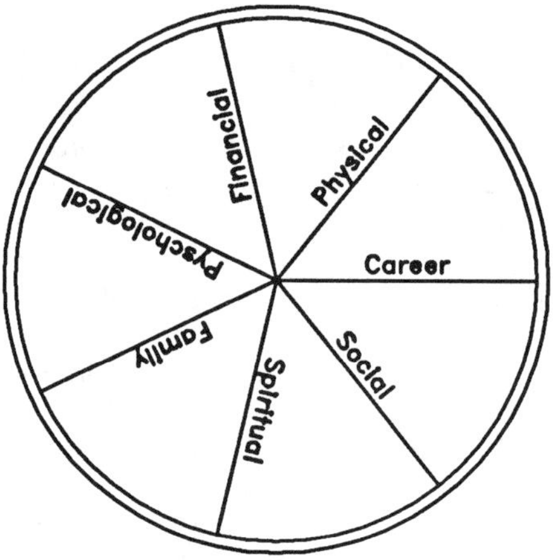

2. "What has prevented you from reaching your goal?" Write down your response.

Your response tells you what you have to work with and will help you understand where you can improve.

3. Are your surroundings at work and home helping you or hindering you?

	Biggest help	Biggest hindrance
Work		
Home		

Organize and synthesize the data

You have already established the purpose or goal and now you are going to gather together everything to find out (a) what you already have, (b) what you will need and (c) what you can get rid of.

When you connected the dots in the "Wheel of success" exercise, you defined the rim of YOUR success wheel.

The questions are, "How well will it roll?", and "what will it take to balance the wheel?"

This is an exercise in checking the balance in your life.

1. You will want to identify the most critical factors you have to work with. Use the "T" chart to list the positive assets you have and the obstacles you are facing.

TABLE 3 A "T" chart

Assets	**Obstacles**

2. Identify both the major asset and the biggest obstacle with an asterisk.
3. Go back to TABLE 2 and identify the spokes with the highest and lowest value. List them under the appropriate headings in TABLE 3.

→ *Test and validate the conclusion*

The best way to check the validity of your present list is to look at where you are investing your time.

A time log can be very helpful. You invest your time in direct proportion to your priority.

When creating your time log (you can do this in many ways), be sure to ask yourself, "Did I spend the greatest amount of my time on the highest priority?" and "Are my priorities and the amount of time I spent on each of them in sync?"

4 . . . Solution . . What is your plan?

In this phase you will want to answer the question: "WHAT ARE YOU GOING TO DO TO REACH THE PURPOSE YOU DESCRIBED IN PHASE 2?"

Gather relevant data

You know your purpose, you know your assets, and you know the obstacles. Now is the time to develop a plan that will allow you to use your assets to overcome the obstacles.

To get started, it will be helpful to respond to the following questions and use TABLE 4 with its prompts to record some ideas.

1. Before any situation changes, you will need to change. List the new growth, knowledge, and skills you will need in order to achieve the purpose.
2. Many people are interested in your success. Make a list of the individuals, companies, and organizations could help you achieve your purpose.
3. Help comes to those who help themselves. List the actions you can you take to begin the process.
4. Changing or getting out of your present environment could help. List the changes you could make in your environment.

This is a time to do some creative thinking. If logic alone would have worked, you would have already succeeded. You will be looking for lots of ideas about things that could be done to achieve your purpose or goal. Be creative.

Look at your situation from another person's point of view:

5. How would the president of a company, government, or research organization solve your problem?
6. Can you identify someone else who experienced a similar problem? How did they solve it?

Can you identify a mentor (A person like the person you would like to become)?

7. How would your mentor solve this problem?

TABLE 4 Personal changes

	Logical	Emotional	Creative
What growth, skills, and knowledge will I need?			
What individuals or companies would help?			
What immediate actions could I take?			
Possible changes in my environment			

Organize and synthesize the data

1. Go back to TABLE 5 and place an "X" in the appropriate column (Logical, Emotional, or Creative) to identify each statement according to type.
2. Look at each of the logical responses you put down and rank them. Put an "H" by the high priority, "M" for moderate priority, and "L" for the low priority.
3. Now go back and rank the "H" priorities numerically. Give the highest priority 1, the second 2, the third 3, etc.
4. Repeat the process for the emotional responses and the creative responses.
5. You are now looking for a statement of priority that meets the #1 priority in each category. It may end up being something you hadn't quite considered. That's OK.
6. Include in your statement both the first thing to do and the most important thing to do.

My plan for reaching my purpose is

___

→ *Test and validate the conclusion*

You are looking for results, but at this point you have only ideas.

Here are a couple of simple ways to check the quality of your plan.

1. Find and talk to your mentor (someone you respect and someone you could confide in). Ask their advice. Lay out some of the facts and ideas and ask the following question: "If you were in my position, what would you do?"
2. Most testing involves some sort of simulation of what you are attempting to do. Could you simulate what could happen if your plan was successfully completed? Is that what you want? If it is, proceed to the next phase. If it isn't, repeat this phase until it is what you want.

5 . . . Design . . How will you implement your solution?

Designs are tools or instruments that help us achieve our goals. We can all use help starting and sticking with our plan, staying on track, staying motivated and having check-points along the way.

In this phase you would want to develop a design that will do just that.

The design will always be made up of two parts: The logical/mechanical part of the design for doing the work, and the emotional/meaning part of the design to help us maintain our attitude and stay motivated. Your design could be as simple as a checklist of your progress or something as radical as changing your entire environment.

Gather relevant data

To look at this from several points of view, we will use two tables:

1. Use TABLE 5 to list some known solutions that address the logical and mechanical process for accomplishing your plan. List the logical solutions to both.
2. A technique I suggest here is to copy and modify. Find something that works, copy and modify it for your own unique situation. Identify what to copy and how to modify it.
3. Work backwards.

TABLE 5 Things to help stay on track

Solutions that could help me do the work

4. Use TABLE 6 to list some known solutions that address the emotional component. (things that could act as reminders and motivators you could incorporate into your design).

TABLE 6 Things to help stay on track

Solutions that could help me stay motivated

Organize and synthesize the data

A helpful technique for prioritizing your designs is to use a decision chart (TABLE 7). This will help you decide which design has the most potential.

1. Use TABLE 7 to list your designs across the top of the matrix (3a, 4a, 5a, etc.)and repeat them down the left side. (3, 4, 5, etc.)
2. Compare Design 1 (#1a) with design 2 (#2a). If you feel that design 1 (#1) is better than design 2 (#2a) fill in a "1" as I did in the example. If it is not better, fill in a "0".
3. Repeat the process for each design you list.
4. Complete the process by totaling across (total the row) and enter the total in the Total column.
5. You now have a list of the designs ranked by potential. Apply this to each category.

TABLE 7 Decision matrix

	1a Design 1	2a Design 2	3a	4a	5a	6a	7a	Total
1 Design 1	0	1						
2 Design 2		0						
3			0					
4				0				
5					0			
6						0		
7							0	

6. You now have identified the design with the most potential, but it still needs to be modified to meet your specific purpose.

7. List the modifications you will want to make.
   a.
   b.
   c.

Describe your design

→ *Test and validate the conclusion*

The only way to test your design ideas is to put them into action.

6 . . . *Evaluating* . . How successful are you ?

It's important to remember that there are many ways to evaluate things. As in design, it's not what it looks like but what it does that counts.

✥ *Gather relevant data*

1. List various points of view that you could use to evaluate your success in the decision matrix below.

TABLE 8 Criteria for evaluation

	Logical	Emotional	Creative

Organize and synthesize the data

1. Identify each point of view as Logical, Emotional, or Creative.
2. Identify the most critical "Logical" point of view.
3. Identify the most critical "Emotional" point of view.
4. Finish this step by filling in your summary statement. This statement should contain both the logical and emotional points of view.

The most important point of view to me is:

____

Test and validate the conclusion

The test is very obvious: Does it do the job you intended?

Yes ____ No ____

CHAPTER 12

Applying the design process to the design of your workspace

This is an exercise in evaluating and redesigning your present workspace.

FIGURE 2 An overview of the design process

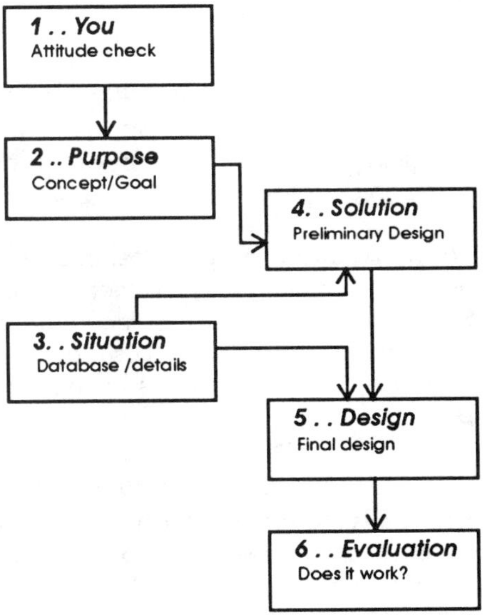

In this phase of the process, you address the issue of WHY you should be personally involved in this project.

You begin this project as you do every project, by checking your attitude, your motives, and your ability to do the work.

This project involves applying the design process (providing organization and meaning) to the design of your workspace.

If you're not interested in this project, you're bored, you're frustrated, you don't want to take the time, or you're unwilling to accept the demands the project will make of you, you will either need to make the necessary changes or stop right now.

It is counter-productive to everyone involved for you to start something that you won't complete.

You limit the success of the project

Keep in mind that you are critical to the success of this project. Your physical, emotional, and spiritual capabilities will be major factors in reaching the project goals. The solutions you seek will never be better than you are.

Success is available to you

Think about how many people have succeeded in designing successful workspaces. There are hundreds. You can do it too.

We could cite example after example of people who had everything going for them in design and failed. Some people think that being in the right place at the right time is the answer to success, and that's partly true but, the real key lies in the person behind the project.

You need a plan

Success is the result of planning. Today only about five percent of people have a plan for their life. Some people think that success in design just happens. But this is seldom the case. Success is the result of opportunity and preparedness coming together. You must be prepared when the opportunity arises, and that takes planning.

Check your attitude

Activity and attitude go together. You don't have one without the other. If you have a positive attitude you will take positive, confident steps toward your goal. Not only that, your enthusiasm will become contagious and others will want to help you.

Check your motives

Check your motives. If this project is directed to helping you help others succeed, you will succeed. If your motives are only self-centered and self-serving, the project will ultimately fail.

Check your self image

As a designer, you have a unique contribution to make. Don't expect your design to be just like everyone else's. It may be scary for you to recognize that you are unique until you recognize that everyone else is unique also. Your uniqueness is exceedingly valuable, so accept it.

Check your commitment level

The challenge lies in getting yourself to do what you know has to be done. Commitment demands a quality decision that says: "I will, until it's done". Once you have made that quality decision, everything becomes focused and easier to achieve. It's easier to be outstanding than it is to be mediocre.

Take this old saying as your project motto. "If it's going to be, it's up to me". The only way you will get this job done is if you do it. No one has more interest in your success than you do. If you are willing to do the menial things necessary, opportunities will come your way.

Work on character

You can't be one kind of person and another kind of designer. Work on your character. Character is far more desirable and difficult to come by than technical skills. Show me someone that is interested in the work, trustworthy, teachable, and trainable, and people will help them to succeed.

You have exactly what you want

Take a good look at yourself. Right now you have exactly the workspace you want. If you didn't want that workspace, you would have been making different decisions. Your present workspace is the result of your past actions.

You may find that you will need to develop new skills to complete this project. These changes will require effort but if you continue to do what you are doing, you will continue to have what you have.

Invest in your strengths

Don't get caught up in thinking someone else can do a better job than you can, and don't waste your time trying to be something that you're not.

Invest your time in doing what you're good at. Do more of what you do well and do it better.

You can change

As long as you have brought your last responsibility to closure, you can always change your direction. Never leave a project before it's completed.

The cowards never begin and the weak will drop out along the way.

Consider possible purposes

Take a few minutes to jot down some of the emotional, logical, and creative reasons it is to your advantage to become personally involved in designing your own workspace.

Some of your reasons might include the fact that you know more about your work than anyone else, it's a challenge, you are working for the payoff, it's an opportunity to practice your profession, or you see an opportunity to help others.

Use TABLE 1 to record some of your reasons.

TABLE 1 Reasons for designing my workspace

	Logical	Emotional	Creative

Organize and synthesize the data

Now take a moment to look at your list. Use the columns at the right of the table and use a check mark to note whether the motive is Logical, Emotional, or Creative. It could be more than one.

A logical reason might be that you know more about your work than anyone else. An emotional motive might be that you feel it's a challenge. A creative motive might be that you want to see if you could make the design without drawings.

Be honest with yourself as you identify your real reason for doing the project. Your motives will usually be obvious to you at this point. You may need to combine two or more statements to make an accurate and complete statement.

I am committed to doing an excellent job!

Test and validate the conclusion

Check to see if you reason is consistent with your time commitments.

Keep your motive in front of you at all times. Write it on a card that you can keep in your pocket.

In phase "1" you addressed WHY "*you*" became involved in the project. In this phase you address WHY the "*project*" needs to be done.

Be clear

The more clearly you can define the purpose of your workspace, the less back-tracking and revising you will need to do later (although there is probably no way of avoiding some back-tracking). You need to make decisions because you are limited in time.

Stay focused

To remain focused on your purpose will require commitment.

Gather relevant data

1. Use the first section of TABLE 1 to develop a menu of possible purposes.

   Have you thought about how what lifestyle will help you accomplish your goals?

   The purpose for doing the project might include any one of the following reasons: To encourage physical fitness while you are working, or to increase the speed of completing projects, or to expand the number of projects you can take on, or to make your workspace a more pleasant environment, or to correct code violations, or to accept a new computer system.

   You might find that the matrix below (Table 2) which is used by designers, is helpful for expanding your thinking about the possible purposes of the project. The categories are quite self-explanatory.

   You can use the "Function" to identify the people involved, the activities that need to be done and the relationships between the activities. "Form" is used to describe the present facility, the building, the furnishings, and their quality. "Economy" is used to describe the economic considerations, and "Time" is used to consider the changes over time.

The columns should be used for entering both *qualitative data* and *quantitative data*. You can see that there's lots to think about. Your limit is simply the amount of time you are willing to invest.

It 's not so much a time to be practical as it's a time to identify possibilities.

2. Use the second section of TABLE 1 to think about and record the assumptions you had to make in generating your list of things you would like to accomplish.

3. Use the last section of TABLE 1 to think about and record what you would do if you accomplished all the items on your list of things you would like your workspace to do.

TABLE 1 List some possible purposes

	Logical	Emotional	Creative
Things I would like my workspace to do			
What assumptions are you making?			

	Logical	Emotional	Creative
What will be your purposes after these?			

TABLE 2 General data for describing the workspace

	Goals	Facts	Concept	Needs
Function people activities relationships				
Form site environ quality				
Economy initial \$ operating \$ life cycle \$				
Time past present future				

Organize and synthesize the data

The purpose for organizing and synthesizing TABLE 1 is to attempt to identify the single most important thing for the workspace to do.

The solution can only address one purpose at a time. If you decide to design your workspace to increase the speed of completing projects, it will not necessarily be the most economical solution, for example.

1. You can begin to reduce the many purposes you listed in TABLE 1 to a single most important purpose by putting a check in the appropriate box indicating whether there is a logical, emotional or creative purpose.
2. Look at each of the logical responses you put down and rank them. Put an "H" by the high priority, "M" for moderate priority, and "L" for the low priority.
3. Now go back and rank the "H" priorities numerically. Give the highest priority 1, the second 2, the third 3, etc. Place the appropriate number after each letter. Your entry might look like "H1" or 'H3"
4. Repeat the process for the emotional responses and the creative responses.
5. Develop a statement of purpose that meets the #1 priority in each category. Don't be surprised if your statement is something you hadn't quite considered. That's OK.
6. Include in your statements both the physical and the emotional purpose.

   One office manager I worked with described his purpose as "giving the most pleasant offices to the individuals who spent the most time in the office". Another manager's purpose was to allow the employees to do their work with the minimum amount of movement and be supportive of the employee's need for privacy.

The single most important purpose of my workspace is:

____

→ ***Test and validate the conclusion***

Take time to really think about your purpose statement and:

1. Check to see if your statement is consistent with your inner FEELINGS.
2. Check the statement with your ACTIONS. You invest your time in direct proportion to your priorities.
3. When you are comfortable with your statement, move on to the next phase.

Give your summary statement to at least 5 people and ask them to tell you what they think it means. When 4 out of 5 people describe the purpose as you intend, then you are ready to continue.

If they do not understand the purpose of the project from your statement, rework this section until you get the desired result.

3 . . . *Situation* ..What do you have to work with?

At this point you have a clear statement of WHY the project is being done. This "situation" phase addresses the issue of WHAT you have to work with.

←↑→↓ *Gather relevant data*

Begin by describing each component or part that makes up this situation.

Describe the existing space, the equipment, the furnishings, and the image that you have to work with. If you have a computer, describe its size, make a scale drawing of it, and describe any design considerations associated with that piece of equipment. For a computer, you might note the concern for glare on the screen, the distances that need to be maintained around the computer, the electrical needs, etc.

Develop a complete inventory in the form of a database. Include yourself in the database.

The matrix (Table 4) is useful for prompting and categorizing the data that you are gathering. Having a clear understanding of what you have will help you understand what you are adding and subtracting in the new design.

TABLE 3 Describing the existing situation

	Goals	**Facts**	**Concept**	**Needs**
Function My activities relationships				
Form site environ quality				

	Goals	Facts	Concept	Needs
Economy initial $ operating $ life cycle $				
Time past present future				

Describe the important relationships that exist between the parts. Using an adjacency chart will be very helpful (Chapter 14, Figure 7).

Describe the activities. Using a flowchart will be very helpful (Chapter 14, Figure 6).

Describe the existing space allocations. Using a block diagram will be very helpful (Chapter 14, Figure 5).

If this database is flawless, it will contain everything that you will need to know in order to complete the project and avoid all irrelevant information. This is, of course, impossible. Nevertheless, it is the goal.

Organize and synthesize the data

Purge your database of everything you don't need to make room for what you will need.

Test and validate the conclusion

You can test the database by asking a question like "What is the size of my desk?" and seeing if the database has the answer.

The real test of the database will be reflected by the amount of time you need to spend running around for information after completing this phase.

4 . . . Solution . . What is the plan?

In this phase you develop a solution for achieving the purpose you identified earlier in the project. You address the issue of WHAT you will do to achieve that purpose.

Develop possible solutions

Determine how much time you have to develop the solution. Divide your time into three segments: A segment for logic techniques; followed by a segment for creative techniques; and finally a logic segment. You want to develop as many ways of achieving the purpose as you can.

Review the purpose statement and the situation database. This will often immediately suggest some possible solutions.

Commit to writing down ten logical solutions for achieving the functional and emotional requirements of the project.

Create an environment that encourages new associations by going to the space you will be designing. Stand in the space and get a feel for it. More ideas will come to your attention. Don't be critical of any idea at this point.

Use some of your creative time to force new associations (innovation is the result of new associations). Use the following matrix (TABLE 4) to force new associations.

1. Under the heading **Concept**, list not less than six concepts or ideas that could be used to achieve the purpose. Some of the concepts could come from the list of ten logical solutions you just developed. These six concepts do not all need to be logical, however. An example is a concept for encouraging physical fitness wile you work might be to have a masseuse or masseur work on you while you work on your work.

   Under the heading **Organization**, list not less than six methods that could you could use to organize your workspace. For example you could organize the equipment based on function and what needs to work together, i.e. --the printer close to the computer. Refer to Methods of organization, Chapter 14 Figure 4 for various methods of organization.

2. Under the heading **Image**, list not less than six possible images the workspace could convey. For example your workspace could look like or remind you of a factory.

TABLE 4 Forcing Associations

Concept	**Organization**	**Image**

3. Select a concept, a method of organization, and an image. Imagine what it would look like. You could imagine your workspace as a paperless office organized around the necessary equipment, which looks like a factory. The possible combinations of associations are enormous (refer to Chapter 14 Figure 10 for an example).

4. Record your solutions by listing them using verbal descriptions, or better yet by using sketches or models of your ideas.

TABLE 5 Solutions list

	Solution description
Solution 1	
Solution 2	
Solution 3	
Solution 4	
Solution 5	
Solution 6	

5. If you need more ideas, combine two ideas to generate another idea.

Back in the purpose phase we gave the example of the supervisor who decided to give the best offices to the people who had to spend the most time on the site. His solution was to locate the conference rooms in the middle of the floor and to surround them with the executive offices and locate the support staff at the perimeter. (draw out your idea of this below):

At this point, you are looking for a number of possible solutions. You are not looking for the best solution. Two mediocre solutions may lead to one good solution.

Organize and synthesize the data

Now you want to look for the solution with the most potential. Use an evaluation chart (Chapter 14 Figure 12) to identify the best solution from the list you just completed. (Table 5)

Be certain that your solution statement describes what is to be included, how the space is to be organized and what image you are attempting to project.

Record the solution knowing that you have other solutions that you can use if this one is not acceptable.

My idea is:

Test and validate the conclusion

If you are satisfied with your solution, continue to the next phase. If not, consider the second idea and if that is unacceptable, go on to the next until you are satisfied.

At this point, you understand the purpose of the project, you have in the database all the necessary data about the project (everything from the drawings of the space to the costs and the legal limitations), you have the solution which describes what is to be included, how the space is to be organized and what image you are attempting to project. You will to break this phase into two parts; THE PRELIMINARY DESIGN and THE FINAL DESIGN.

THE PRELIMINARY DESIGN

The preliminary design is used to verify the acceptance of the direction the design is taking in carrying out the solution.

Develop possible designs

Work from the general to the specific.

1. Identify the major areas that must be included in the space. These could include the conference area, the computer area, the file area, the entryway, and so on.
2. Develop each area as a "block" which will make up a block diagram. In order to define the size of the block, you will need to define each subarea that will make up that block.
3. Develop several block diagrams which could meet the organization requirements of the solution. These block diagrams will clearly describe the size and relationship of the various areas. If the solution is related to time, you might describe the solution in terms of a flowchart.
4. Develop several images that could meet the image requirements of the solution.

Organize and synthesize the data

Use the evaluation chart technique described in Chapter 14 Figure 12 to identify the best block diagram and the best image for meeting the solution requirements.

Test and validate the conclusion

Your satisfaction of the block diagram and the image determines the success of the preliminary design.

THE FINAL DESIGN

The final design phase is used for the final detailing and approval of the design before the specifications are assembled and the design is constructed.

Develop possible final designs

1. Apply the block diagram to the existing space. You will find that you need to make modifications to both the block diagram and the space.

   If the space doesn't exist, begin with a square and start to modify it, adding where more space is necessary and chopping off corners where they are not necessary to meet the needs.

   Remember that no two situations are ever alike. Even if the task is the same, the people are different.

2. Select equipment and furnishings that fit and please you. This is your workspace. Forget about what anybody else thinks. This space is unique to you (you may have to consider how your workspace affects the attitude of the public if they need to have access to your office).

3. After developing each of the major areas, determine the relationships within each major area and each sub-area.

   As you relate one sub-area to another you will often find that the subareas need to be modified. Be careful to make the modifications without losing sight of your purpose and your solution.

4. It is likely that you will make additional changes when you take into consideration the 3-dimensional space.

   It is very helpful to begin by thinking about the space as having three levels: A floor space; a midair space; and a ceiling space. Locate things on their appropriate level (you will find that the two-dimensional flat arrangements offer far less options than three-dimensional arrangements).

Allow your design to evolve. Enjoy the changes that are brought about because of additional requirements. This is like watching a Victorian house evolve over time. You add some here, subtract some there, and the result is fascinating.

5. Test often by imagining yourself working an entire day in the new space. This is when you begin to realize that you have more to design. Where is the telephone? What is that distraction? Where is my window?

   Start to take control of the space in your imagination. Start removing any restrictions and adding things you see that you need. What would help you work better, faster, cheaper, healthier, etc.? Sketch the ideas and draw out the plans.

6. Fill in the colors and the textures in your imagination.

7. When you are satisfied, record the images.

8. Do it again, and again. Give yourself at least 3 different designs to choose from. If you only have one design, you don't have any choice.

9. Label or number each design.

Organize and synthesize the data

Use the evaluation chart technique described in Chapter 14 Figure 12 to identify the best design for meeting the solution requirements.

Test and validate the conclusion

It's very helpful to let the design evolve by constructing some of the design, living with it and then constructing more, living with it a while longer, and doing some more. You might begin by bringing in some of the moveable furniture and using it a while before constructing cabinets.

10. Having selected a design, you are ready to loop back in the design process and design the support systems (such as the lighting and electrical systems).

11. When the decisions are complete, you are ready to prepare the specifications for the project. This includes drawings and written descriptions of what is to be included in the design and how the design is to be assembled. These specifications are a legal document.

12. Contracts would then be developed and the construction would begin.

I firmly believe that a project such as this should never be complete. Your work will change, you will change, and the space will want to change. Change is the motivator in life.

What the design does for you is more important than what it looks like.

We come to value the things that help us. We did that with both the horseless carriage, the submarine, and the bicycle. Can you imagine getting someone excited about the idea of balancing on two wheels and going down the road? The first question would be, "Can it be done?" followed by "Who would want to?" We have come to appreciate the bicycle and it's still around today.

On the other hand, we rid ourselves of things that do not help or no longer serve their intended function, such as the washboard, the trolley car (except in San Francisco), and the bustle.

List various points of view

You could evaluate your design from many points of view. You could look at it from the point of view of initial cost, return on investment, image, efficiency, effectiveness, and so forth. List the many points of view you could have in evaluating the design of your workspace.

TABLE 6 Points of view

View 1	
View 2	
View 3	
View 4	
View 5	
View 6	
View 7	
View 8	
View 9	

Organize and synthesize the data

1. Use a matrix to identify the most significant point of view for evaluating your work space.

TABLE 7 Evaluation Decision Matrix

	View 1	View 2	View 3	View 4	View 5	Total
View 1						
View 2						
View 3						
View 4						
View 5						

The most important evaluation criteria is:

____

Test and validate the conclusion

The most significant point of view should be consistent with the purpose you developed early in the project.

Does the design help you or hinder you?

CHAPTER 13

Applying the design process to design of your career

1..You... What's your attitude about doing this project?

In this phase of the process, you address the issue of WHY you should be personally involved in this project.

You begin this project as you do every project, by checking your attitude, your motives, and your ability to do the work.

This project involves applying the design process (providing organization and meaning) to the design of your career.

If you're not interested in this project, you're bored, you're frustrated, you don't want to take the time, or you're unwilling to accept the demands the project will make of you, you will either need to make the necessary changes or stop right now.

It is counter-productive to everyone involved for you to start something that you won't complete.

You limit the success of the project

Keep in mind that you are critical to the success of this project. Your physical, emotional, and spiritual capabilities will be major factors in reaching the project goals. The solutions you seek will never be better than you are.

Success is available to you

It doesn't matter what profession you look at. Every profession has its successes and its failures. Think about that. The key to success is not in the choice of profession. You will find that it has little to do with education, intellect, or background. It has everything to do with maximizing what you have to work with.

You could cite example after example of people who had everything going for them and failed, and at the same time you could find example after example of people with seemingly nothing going for them who succeeded. Some people think that being in the right place at the right time is the answer and that's partly true but, the real key lies in the people.

You need a plan

Success is the result of planning. Today only about five percent of the people have a plan for their career. Some people think that success just happens. But this is seldom the case. Success is the result of opportunity and preparedness coming together. You must be prepared when the opportunity arises, and that takes planning.

Check your attitude

Activity and attitude go together. You don't have one without the other. If you have a positive attitude you will take positive, confident steps toward your goal. Not only that, your enthusiasm will become contagious and others will want to help you.

Check your motives

Check your motives. If you direct your attention to helping a company succeed, you will succeed. If your motives are only self-centered and self-serving (if you are simply looking for a job), the job will elude you.

Check your self image

As a person, you have a unique contribution to make. Don't expect it to be just like everyone else's. It may be scary for you to recognize that you are unique until you recognize that everyone else is unique also. Your uniqueness is exceedingly valuable, so accept it. Don't be intimidated by others' comments.

Check your commitment level

The challenge lies in getting yourself to do what you know has to be done. Finding the best place to work take commitment. Commitment demands a quality decision that says: "I will, until it's done". Once you have made that quality decision, everything becomes focused and easier to achieve. It's easier to be outstanding than it is to be mediocre.

Take this old saying as your project motto. "If it's going to be, it's up to me". No one can interview for you. The only way you will get this job is if you go out and get it. No one has as much interest in your success as you do. If you are willing to do the menial things it takes to complete the task, opportunities will come your way.

Work on character

You can't be one kind of person and another kind of employee or professional. Work on your character. Character is far more desirable to a company and far more difficult to come by than technical skills. Show me someone that is interested in the work, trustworthy, teachable, and trainable, and companies will impel them to success.

You have exactly what you want

Take a good look at yourself. Right now you have exactly what you want. If you didn't want what you now have you would have been making different decisions. Your present position in life is the result of your past actions.

You may find that you will need to develop more skills to get the position you want. Changes always require effort, but if you continue to do what you are doing, you will continue to have what you have. Be willing to make the changes.

Invest in your strengths

Don't get caught up in thinking the grass is greener on the other side of the fence, it's not. Don't waste your time trying to be something that you're not. Invest your time in doing what you're good at. Do more of what you do well and do it better.

You can change

As long as you have brought your last responsibility to closure, you can change your direction. You can take the skills you learned and apply them to other area, but never leave a project before it's completed.

The cowards never begin and the weak will drop out along the way.

Gather relevant data

Take a few minutes to jot down some of the emotional, logical, and creative reasons it is to your advantage to become personally involved in designing your career.

Some of your reasons might include the fact that only you could do the work, it's a challenge, you are working for the payoff, or you see an opportunity to help others.

Use TABLE 1 to record some of your reasons.

TABLE 1 Some motives for designing my career

	Logical	Emotional	Creative

Organize and synthesize the data

Now take a moment to look at your list. Use the columns at the right of the table and use a check mark to note whether the motive is Logical, Emotional, or Creative. It could be more than one.

A logical reason might be that only you could do the work. An emotional reason might be that it's a challenge. A creative motive might be that you want to see if you could make a game out of your life plan.

Be honest with yourself as you identify your real reason for doing the project. Your motives will usually be obvious to you at this point. You may need to combine two or more statements to make an accurate and complete statement.

I am committed to doing an excellent job!

____

Test and validate the conclusion

Check to see if you reason is consistent with your time commitments.

Keep your motive in front of you at all times. Write it on a card that you can keep in your pocket, and review it consistently; before interviews, when looking in the classifieds for new opportunities, or when evaluating your current position.

2. *Purpose.* What is the purpose of this project?

In phase "1" you addressed WHY *"you"* became involved in the project. In this phase you address WHY the *"project"* needs to be done.

Be clear

The more clearly you can define the purpose of your career, the easier it will be to achieve. You will have to make choices and focus your attention.

You can be outstanding in some areas too, but not every area. Because of time constraints, you will need to make choices.

Stay focused

To remain focused on your purpose will require commitment.

The big picture

Get a global view of what needs to be done and identify what you would be willing to do.

Many people think the purpose of this type of project is to find a job. It's more than that. It's identifying the contribution you can make, planning a lifestyle, and identifying the career or profession that will support that lifestyle. Although your career is not your life, it is a major factor in it.

Thinking about supporting a life style is not self-centered. The better you function, the better you can do your job. In fact, top corporations know that the better you function outside the job, the better you will function on the job.

It always involves people

Everything goes back to people's co-dependency. We are more powerful as a team than as individuals. It takes teamwork to get things done today. Could you grow the cotton, weave the fabric, design, and sew together the shirt or blouse you are wearing? Could you have built the computer you are using? Probably not. We are dependent on each other. You are needed. No man is an "I" land.

Attend to others

You must direct your attention outside of yourself. You can have everything you want if you are willing to help enough other people get what they want. The demand is for the person who is willing to give. The system favors the performer, not the rider.

Gather relevant data

To arrive at a statement of the real purpose for your career, you would want to take a few minutes to develop a menu of possible purposes.

Your purpose might be to be the best in your profession, or to find the fastest growing profession.

1. Use the first section of TABLE 1 to list some of the things that you would like to accomplish.

   Have you thought about how what lifestyle will help you accomplish your goals?

   It's not so much a time to be practical as it's a time to search within to identify what's really in your heart. Search for things that are worthy, that give you a sense of worth, that you could love, and that would allow people to love you for.

   The idea here is to think about your life and its possibilities from as many points of view as you can.

2. Use the second section of TABLE 1 to think about and record the assumptions you had to make in generating your list of things you would like to accomplish.

3. Use the last section of TABLE 1 to think about and record what you would do if you accomplished all the items on your list of things you would like to accomplish.

TABLE 1 List some possible purposes

	Logical	Emotional	Creative
List some things you would like to accomplish			
What assumptions are you making?			
What will be your purposes after these?			

Organize and synthesize the data

The purpose for organizing and synthesizing TABLE 1 is to develop a statement that describes what you want to have happen. This purpose statement is your mission statement or your goal statement.

As you develop this statement of purpose you will find that some detail, important to the project, but distracting to the concept, will come to mind. It might be the need return someone's phone call, for example.

To avoid losing any significant details and avoid being distracted from identifying the real purpose of the project, write down every significant detail that comes to you. Later you can locate it in the database you will be developing in the "Situation" phase of the process.

1. You can begin to reduce the many purposes you listed in TABLE 1 to a single most important purpose by putting a check in the appropriate box indicating whether there is a logical, emotional or creative conclusion.
2. Look at each of the logical responses you put down and rank them. Put an "H" by the high priority, "M" for moderate priority, and "L" for the low priority.
3. Now go back and rank the "H" priorities numerically. Give the highest priority 1, the second 2, the third 3, etc. Place the appropriate number after each letter. Your entry might look like "H1" or 'H3"
4. Repeat the process for the emotional responses and the creative responses.
5. Develop a statement of purpose that meets the #1 priority in each category. Don't be surprised if your statement is something you hadn't quite considered. That's OK.
6. Write the statement down.

Your career statement would want to involve you in something of worth, something worthy of your attention, something that allows you to be loved, and something that gives you a sense of accomplishment.

The single most important purpose of my career is:

____

→ Test and validate the conclusion

Take time to really think about your purpose statement and:

1. Check to see if your statement is consistent with your inner FEELINGS.
2. Check the statement with your ACTIONS. You invest your time in direct proportion to your priorities.
3. When you are comfortable with your statement, move on to the next phase.
4. Give your summary statement to at least 5 people and ask them to tell you what they think it means. When 4 out of 5 people describe the purpose as you intend, then you are ready to continue.

If they do not understand the purpose of the project from your statement, rework this section until you get the desired result.

Gather data not a job

This is not the time to look for a job now. You are gathering information. This is the time to find out what's available. You need to know what there is to work with. This will demand broadening your horizons. The more you do this, the more motived you will become. You will find yourself motivated again and again by the possibilities that exist out there.

In this process many people just spend their time doing the mechanics of this task. Make sure you take the time to time assimilate and understand the bigger picture.

Know what you are getting into

Most graduates accept the first or the second job that's offered. They accept the job not because they know what it's all about, but out of fear that's the only offer they will get. I personally know students who went through four years of college without ever talking to someone who was doing what they thought they wanted to do. They got their degree and accepted a job in their chosen profession only to find out they didn't like it. That's not the time to find you don't like it. The time is now!

Practice talking to people

Of the many ways of getting a job, nothing is better than talking to people who are doing what you want to do. You can read about companies, you can listen to the recruiters from a company, but nothing beats talking to the people who are doing the job. It gives you insight that you cannot get from the personnel office. You also cannot get the people you need to talk with through the personnel office. You need to go to them directly, not for a job, but for information. Make a friend. A friend in your chosen profession is far more valuable than even the information.

Will they talk with me?

Your chosen "mentor" will talk with you if you respect their time. You are asking to talk with a person about their favorite subject: themselves. You will be one of the very few people who has shown an interest in them.

What if they won't talk with you? That's simple too. If they are rude to a guest, they are likely to be more rude with their co-workers. You don't want to be there anyway. Find someone else. Don't take it personally. If you keep this up you will be rewarded with the recognition that "like attracts like". If you like the company or person, the company or person will like you.

The 80/20 rule

It has been said that in any organization, eighty percent of the people are riders, while only twenty percent are the performers doing the work. It's also been said eighty percent of the people do twenty percent of the work while twenty percent of the people do eighty percent of the work. Which one would you want to hire? I think the answer is obvious. Here's the question. How do I get in the performers group? It's a choice. Choose to be the performer. The system favors the performer.

Overcoming fear

You must overcome fear. Here's the key: Direct your attention to the other person. You can concentrate on one thing only at a time. Either you are concentrating on others or you are concentrating on yourself. Success comes when you focus your attention outward. Fear comes when you focus your attention inward.

The help from others

Many of us find it easier to help others than to receive help ourselves. We all need help. Don't hesitate in accepting it when it's available. You will most likely get your position based on someone else's recommendation. Not because you are so terrific, but because of trust people have in the person who recommended you and the trust that person has in you.

You repay them by living up to their recommendation and trust, so that the person who hired you says to the person who recommended you, "I really want to thank you for recommending this person." That's the thank you. Some day you can do it for someone else.

Gather relevant data

There are lot's of ways to get the information you will need. Here are a few.

1. Go to the library and read about your own chosen profession.
2. Go to presentations given by people in your chosen profession.
3. Use low risk interviews to network.
    - Talk to people who are doing what you want to do.
    - Make friends with people in your profession.
4. Ask for assistance.
    - Who do they know who is doing what you want to do?
5. Read books on networking and working with people.
6. Volunteer your time to help.
7. Look at your chosen profession as an outsider and see how your profession could benefit others.

Organize and synthesize the data

An excellent place to start is with a 'Data gathering interview' where you set up a meeting with someone who is doing what you think you want to do.

Ask them about what they do, what they like, what they don't like, what they see in the future, what education or training is necessary to do what they do, etc.

The purposed outcome of this process is to make a friend, or at the very least, to decide whether that profession is one in which you'd like to be.

Test and validate the conclusion

Find a need

The plan is to identify an area of need and fill it. Have you ever been in a situation of need? I remember arriving at the emergency room of our local hospital because I had a problem. I had a need.

Be the answer

The young doctor in the emergency room was an answer to the need. I didn't take time to check out the credentials, I didn't ask how much it would cost. I had a need and he was my answer. You can be the answer to someone's problem, you just need to find that problem.

Look for a starting place

You have a plan. You are looking for a place to start. If you do well in this first job, other opportunities will follow. Your first job doesn't necessarily have to be your career.

Start with the best company you can find. Think of it as your training ground. Better to work with the best for less, than to work for a poor company and make more, have the title etc. The first position is an extension of your education. Be confident in where you begin. You will need to make other moves.

Timing is critical

Always remember that things change. You may be ahead of the opportunity time or you may be behind it. Be patient, and wait for your opportunity.

Gather relevant data

1. Research the companies.
2. Return to the people you did information gathering interviews with and ask their advice about companies.
3. Prepare to be the answer to the problem.
4. Develop a relationship with the people you are meeting. Trust is a key word.
5. Keep doing more of what you have been doing.

Organize and synthesize the data

The most important solution is to develop a trusting relationship with the people you meet.

Test and validate the conclusion

People will welcome you.

It's not a game

In a game there is a winner and a loser. Here you are looking for a match. We both win, or we both lose.

Boyfriend/Girlfriend

Finding the right job is like finding the right mate. It's difficult to do it through the mail.

Everyone will be unqualified for the position except one. One is all you need. Don't get discouraged by the word NO. NO simply means "keep going".

Here's a way to think about this. If I picked off the street the first ten people of your opposite sex, how many would you go out with? All? Two? None?

Some career positions require spending more time on the job than you will spend with your spouse. If you were to look for a person who you would be willing to spend more time with than you would spend with a spouse, at random, how many people would we have to find to locate one that would qualify? One hundred? Everyone should agree that it will take a lot of looking to find the job that will qualify for you.

That's the process you are involved in. This is going to take time and effort. The payoff will be worth it! You will want to look for your "ideal career".

Gather relevant data

1. Check off the interviews
2. Keep track of your results
3. Record the results in a matrix

Organize and synthesize the data

Identify the opportunity that will put you in the best position for your next move. This will help you stay properly motivated so that you can do the job with anticipation rather than frustration.

Use a decision-making matrix (Chapter 14, figure 11) and develop the criteria for evaluating the opportunities. What must the job do? What else would you want it to do?

Score the matrix.

Identify the opportunity that meets your highest logical and emotional needs.

Test and validate the conclusion

Do you have a good feeling about the opportunity you are selecting?

*6 . . . Evaluation . .*A job review after 1 year

It will take about a year to know how successful you have been. It will take about two years to prove you are qualified for the job you've accepted.

Gather relevant data

Some of the ways you could evaluate the job
1. Sense of satisfaction.
2. Positioning for the next opportunity.
3. Co-workers.
4. Experience.
5. Finances.
6. Performance.

Organize and synthesize the data

What is most is important to you about your perspective job?

Test and validate the conclusion

Are you excited about the results you're getting?

CHAPTER 14 *Visuals*

FIGURE 1 Design Skills

The design process involves the cycling of three skills. The skills of gathering data, synthesizing the data, and validating the data are skills that are shared by every profession.

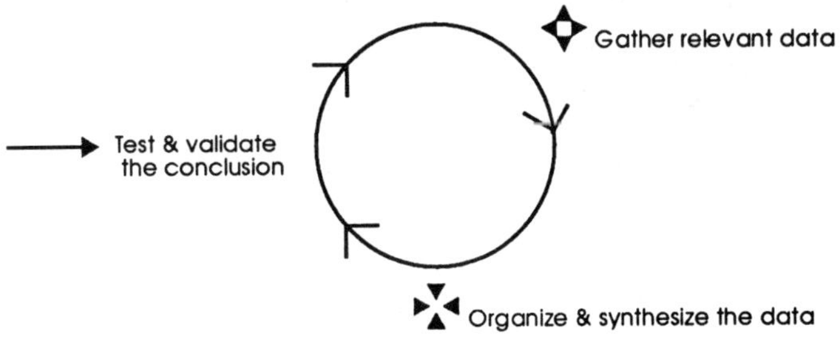

FIGURE 2 — The effect of time on the design process

The design process spirals as it moves through time. It never returns to the same place. Everything that you target will have moved by the time you get there.

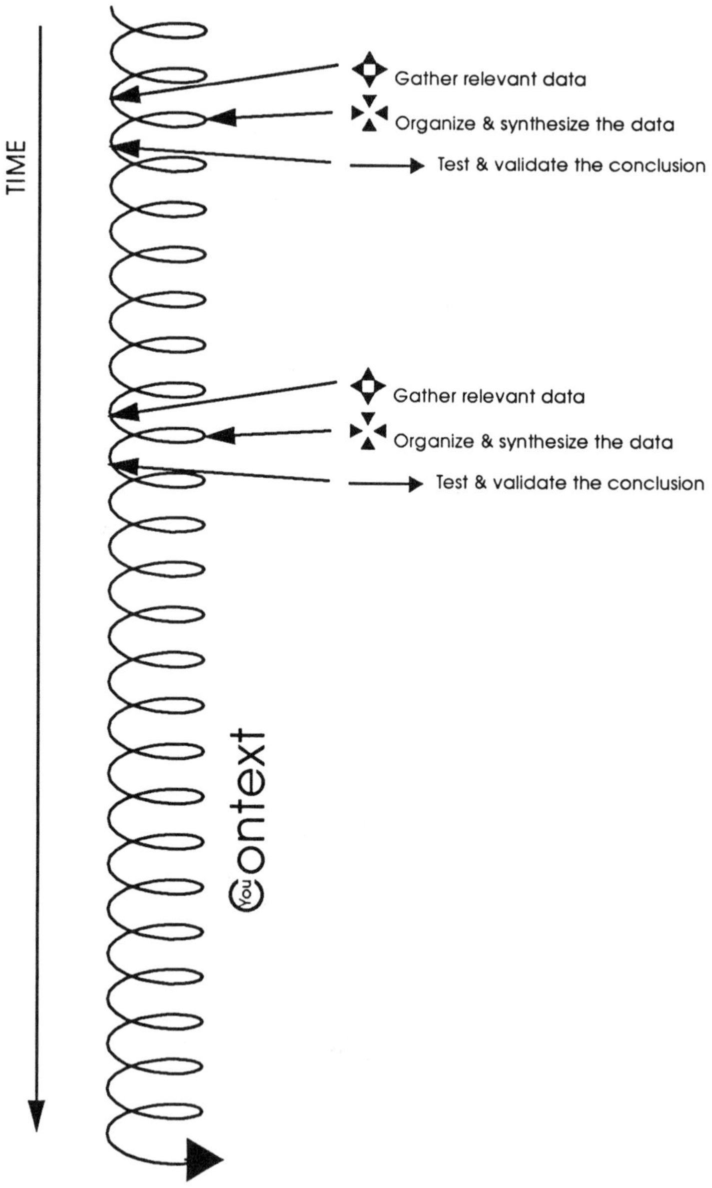

FIGURE 3 General Systems Language

The general systems language is a convenient method for envisioning a bigger picture.

For example, if you choose to stop the manufacture of aircraft, a decision at the level of Society, the result will be changes at every other level.

You will see job loss at the Community level, stress in the Family, etc.

GENERAL SYSTEMS LANGUAGE

Universe		
Solar system		
Biosphere	⟶	Improve air quality
Humankind		
Society	⟵	Stop the manufacture of aircraft
Culture		
Sub-culture		
Community	⟶	Loss of jobs
Family	⟶	Stress in the family
Individual	⟶	Stress in the family
Biosystem		
Organs	⟶	Signs and symptoms of disease
Tissues		
Cells		
Organelles		
Molecules		
Atoms		
Subatomic particles		
Non-mass energy		

FIGURE 4 Methods of organization

Traditionally designers will use one or more of the following options for organizing objects in space.

Organizing the function relationships

SEQUENCE	GROUPS
Priority	Density
Importance	Service central/non-central
Hierarchy	Activity Integrated/non Int.
Authority	People Individual/group
Flow	Home Territory
Flexibility	Relationship
Phasing	Communication
	Neighbors
	Accessible
	Separate flow
	Mixed flow
	Orientation
	Tolerance Tailored/loose
	Safety
	Energy conserve.
	Envir. control
	Cost control

FIGURE 5 A block diagram

A block diagram is used to describe the size and relationship of the parts of the design.

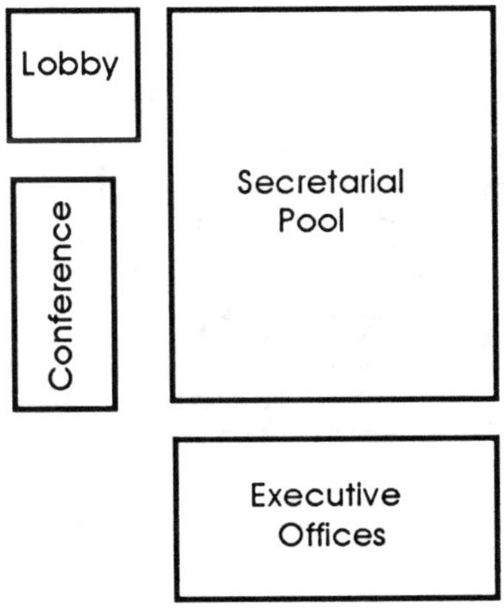

FIGURE 6 An organization chart

An organization chart describes the reporting relationship within an organization.

You will find that the organization chart is often used as the basis for the office layout.

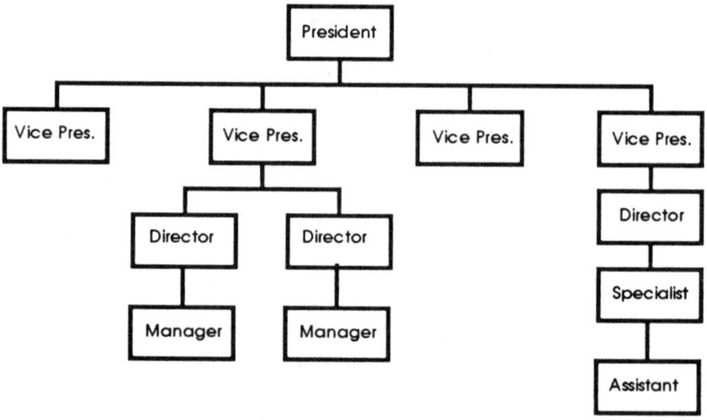

FIGURE 7 An adjacency chart

An adjacency chart is used to describe the importance of the relationship of one space to another.

In this example we will use 3 if the adjacency is very important, 2 if the adjacency is moderately important, and 1 if the adjacency is not important. We will use negative numbers to indicate that the adjacency should not take place.

We begin by comparing the proximity of the Lobby to the Restrooms. In this example we will regard this as very favorable (3). We then compare the Lobby to the Receptionist. We will regard this as also very favorable (3). We then compare the Lobby to the Supervisor and regard this as not important (1). Next we compare the Lobby with the Supervisor and regard this as also not important (1). Finally we compare the Lobby with the Accountant and regard this as highly undesirable (-3). We would then move on the compare the Restrooms to the Receptionist. Let's give this a rating of (2). You would go on the finish the chart.

This is most useful when a summary statement is made and then translated into a block diagram.

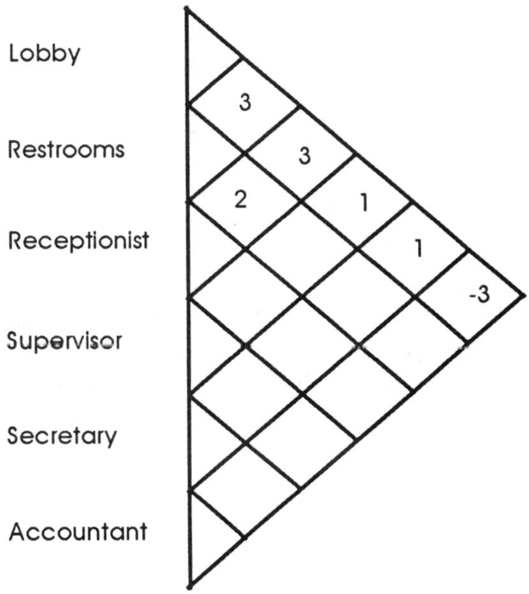

FIGURE 8 A flow chart

A flow chart is very useful to describe a sequence of events including decisions.

The following symbols are useful.

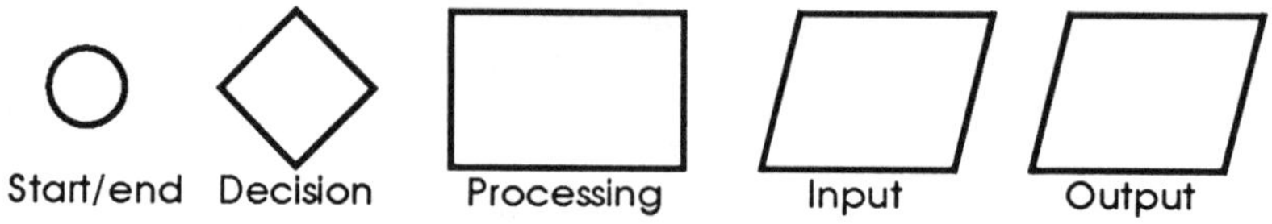

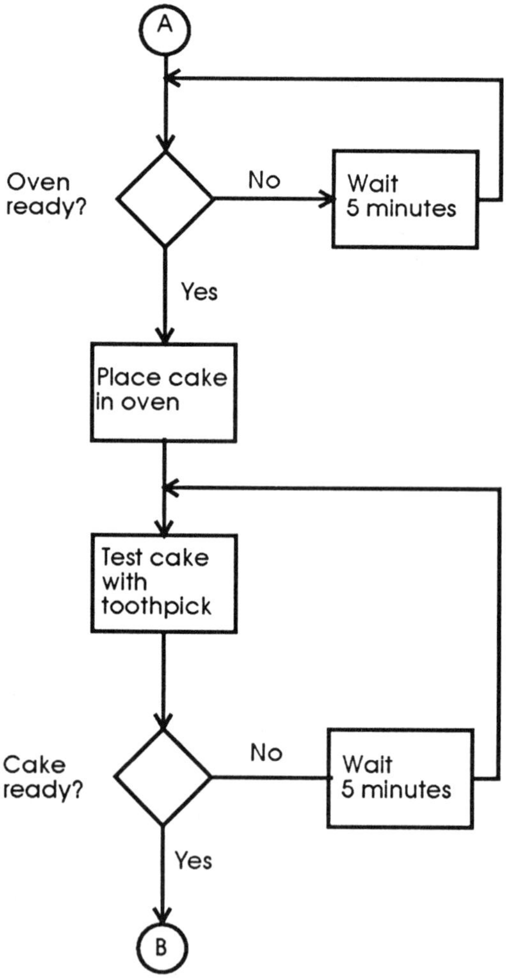

Mind Mapping

Mind mapping is a the technique that is very helpful for outlining materials. It suggests that you draw out your notes rather than outline them in the traditional manner.

Since all memory techniques involve visual images, this technique helps you remember things by generating a visual image.

Begin by imagining that you are drawing a tree and that as you progress you will be drawing the leaves and the branches.

Be creative. Use color, change line weights, change the images. The more unusual the image, the easier it is to remember. Here is an example of a mind mapping sketch.

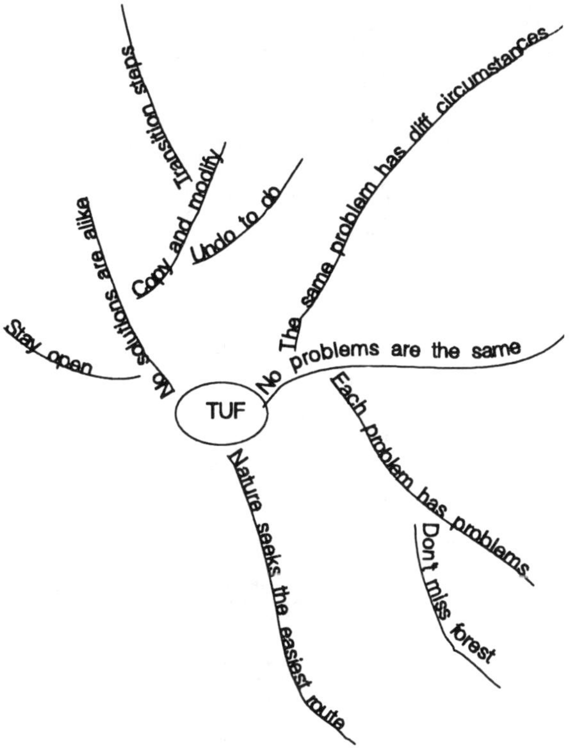

FIGURE 10 Generating forced associations

Forcing associations is a very helpful technique for expanding your thinking.

In this example we will force new associations about an office.

1. Begin by identifying the major parts of the space that you might want to consider. You might include the floor, the ceiling, the walls, the image, the storage, etc.
2. Construct a matrix with one column for each part you are including. Label each column as shown.
3. Now generate options for each category. These options do not need to be either logical or related to the project you are designing. In fact it's best if the options are unusual. Refer to the example below.

   You can generate as many options as you like for each column. The number of options in each column can vary.

4. Select one option from each category and visualize what that office might look like. You might consider an office with a brick floor, a wood ceiling, and glass walls. The office looks like a park and has everything stored in boxes.

   Try this one: The office has a glass floor, the ceiling is sky, and the walls are trees. The image is of a factory and all the storage is hidden.

   The number of possible combinations is amazing. You will have more ideas than you have time to even consider.

Floor	**Ceiling**	**Walls**	**Image**	**Storage**
grass	plaster	glass	factory	shelves
wood	wood	panel	park	boxes
brick	sky	plaster	home	hidden
carpet	acoustic	trees	beach	files

FIGURE 11 A decision chart

This decision chart is very helpful for comparing one item in the list with each of the others and ranking the results. The example below is for one list only.

1. Begin by listing the items you are going to compare both in a column at the left of the matrix and across the top of the matrix.
2. Score each item in the column by comparing it to each item listed across the top. Since **Cost** references itself, the cell is blackened to indicate that no value is required. If **Cost** (in the column) is more important than ***Function***, listed across the top, enter a "1" on the **Cost** ROW (Horizontal line) in the ***Function*** COLUMN (Vertical listing). Use only "0" or "1".
3. Continue scoring **Cost** by comparing it to ***Image*** listed across the top. If **Cost** is less important than ***Image*** listed across the top, enter a "0" on the **Cost** ROW (Horizontal line) in the ***Image*** COLUMN (Vertical listing).
4. Continue making the comparisons in order to complete the matrix.

	Cost	***Function***	***Image***	***Maintenance***	***Safety***	**Total**
Cost	■	1	0			
Function		■				
Image			■			
Maintenance				■		
Safety					■	

5. Total the numbers for **Cost** from left to right and enter the total in the **Total** column.
6. Continue the process for each of the items in the column.
7. The most important point of view is the view with the highest score.

This technique can be used for any list of items.

FIGURE 12 An evaluation chart

This chart is very helpful for including both the logical and emotional components in your selection.

1. Begin developing the criteria for evaluating your ideas by first listing the things the idea must do. List these criteria across the top of the matrix. In my example I am indicating that the idea must be a workspace.
2. Complete a list of what the idea must do. Be careful to list them in their order of importance.
3. Next develop a list of the things that you would like them to do, following the procedure you just completed. Be careful to list these in their order of importance after the "The idea must" list.
4. You can identify the best idea by identifying the idea that meets the most criteria from left to right without missing one.

	Workspace					
	The idea must.			**I want the idea to:**		
Idea 1						
Idea 2						
Idea 3						
Idea 4						
Idea 5						

FIGURE 13 Red flags

Things to remember:

- Don't begin designing until you know what the problem is.
- Don't solve someone else's problem as if it is your own.
- Design cannot be used effectively to motivate an unmotivated person.
- Design cannot be used effectively to solve a management problem.
- The decisions you make will never be better than the data you base them on.
- Until you can explain the situation in simple terms, you probably don't understand it.
- Focus on solutions. Problems will present themselves.
- Develop solutions that feed or encourage the behavior you want to have happen and discourage or starve the behaviors you don't want.
- Just because you haven't seen it before doesn't make it wrong.
- The only security you have is in your ability to perform the work